# Comprehension: Knowledge to Practice

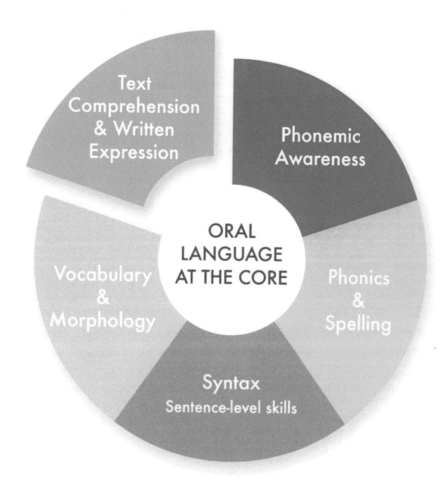

## Margie Bussmann Gillis &
## Nancy Chapel Eberhardt

Literacy**how**
Professional Learning Series

Cover by Liang Design

**Other titles in the Literacy How Professional Learning Series:**
Phonemic Awareness and Phonics: Knowledge to Practice
Vocabulary: Knowledge to Practice
Syntax: Knowledge to Practice
Available at www.amazon.com

The **Literacy How Professional Learning Series** is dedicated to:

The educational researchers whose work informs our understanding;
The Literacy How Mentors who empower teachers
by translating evidence-based knowledge into classroom practice;
The teachers who tirelessly strive to ensure that every child learns to read;
And the students who are at the heart of all that we do.

# Table of Contents

Introduction to the Literacy How Professional Learning Series

## Linking What We Know to What We Do

Literacy How is a professional development organization that has drawn on decades of research to create a current and comprehensive model of how children learn to read. The **Literacy How Professional Learning Series** translates that model into a set of reference and instructional tools for teachers and educators dedicated to developing children's literacy skills. This series links what we know about *how* students acquire literacy skills to evidence-based instructional practices that help them achieve those skills. While the series emphasizes Pre-K-3 conceptual and skill development, teachers of older emerging or struggling readers will also find these reference tools useful.

## The Literacy How Reading Model

The purpose of the Literacy How reading model is to provide a framework for conveying all the elements of literacy required for a child to become a reader, a writer, and a speaker. The Literacy How Reading Wheel below graphically represents those elements. The model builds on the work of Louisa Moats (1999) and the findings of the National Reading Panel (2000). Importantly, it features a core emphasis on oral language in recognition that a young child's oral language skills provide the foundation for all aspects of literacy development. In this regard, the Literacy How reading model goes beyond the National Panel recommendations and includes spelling, syntax, and written expression as significant elements of literacy education.

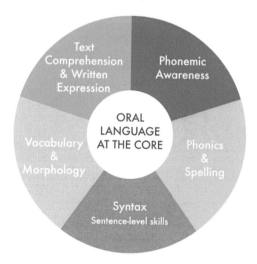

You may notice that fluency, one of the recommendations of the NRP report, is missing from the Literacy How Reading Wheel. That is because the Literacy How model views fluency as essential to all aspects of literacy development. Fluent (i.e., automatic) performances in both discrete and complex literacy tasks are the mark of proficient readers and writers.

## Stages of Reading Development

The Literacy How Reading Wheel represents the content of reading instruction but does not delineate the specific elements that should be taught at various developmental levels. We decided it was important to orient the content on typically developing children. For this, we turned to Chall's stages of reading development (Chall, 1983). Stages 0-2 provide a map of students' progression on the road to skilled reading. Key research findings for each stage assist in determining, evaluating, and developing instruction.

The following table displays the three stages of reading development that serve as an organizational framework for the research, activities, and text-based lessons in the Literacy How Professional Learning Series. As with any aspect of child development, students progress at various rates through the stages, some in a lockstep and sequential manner while others follow a nonlinear route. Regardless of the pace and path, the stages can guide the instructional process.

### Chall's Stages of Reading Development

|  | Stage 0 | Stage 1 | Stage 2 |
|---|---|---|---|
| Name | Pre/early reading | Alphabetic | Consolidation |
| Description | Pre-reading/pretend reading stage: Children learn to recognize and write the letters of the alphabet. The acquisition of phonological awareness is a major development. | Initial reading and decoding stage: Children learn that speech sounds map on to letters to make words and that these words can be read by sounding out each letter or letter's associated sound. | Confirmation and automaticity: Children consolidate their reading skills –decoding, sight word recognition, and comprehension of words and text – and read with increasing fluency. |
| Oral language layer | Oral language, both receptive and expressive, is the foundation for phonological awareness, as well as background information and vocabulary. | Syntactic awareness and syntactic knowledge contribute to reading. By grade 1, most children have sufficient knowledge of syntax for reading. Most also have a sufficiently large listening and speaking vocabulary. (Chall, p. 62) | The language of most children is sufficient for their reading. |
| Approximate Grade (age) | Pre-K (3-5) | K-2 (5-7) | 2-3 (7-9) |
| Focus | Alphabetic Principle Oral Language | Decoding Encoding | Automaticity Prosody |
| Reading component(s) | Listening Comprehension, PA, Invented Writing | | Reading Comp Written Expression |
|  |  | Basic Phonics | Advanced Phonics |
|  | Vocabulary and syntax throughout | | |
| Text type focus that students read | Predictable | Decodable/hybrid | Familiar text, literature, informational text |

## Effective Instructional Practices

All aspects of this series are shaped by the use of effective, evidence-based instructional practices. Researchers have identified effective practices to teach literacy concepts and skills, among which are the following:

1. Explicit instruction
2. Emphasis on making abstract concepts concrete
3. Emphasis on automaticity
4. Development of metacognitive strategies to facilitate transfer of knowledge and skills
5. Stress on cumulative, systematic, and sequential presentation of content and skills
6. Use of data to guide instruction

## Types of Text

Just as the content of reading instruction depends on the age/stage of the child, so too does the type of text used for instruction. Early childhood teachers use predictable texts because they are based on oral language patterns and structures – that is, they are characterized by repeated words and phrases that children can easily remember. Another kind of text, code-emphasis, provides students who understand that sounds map onto letters with an opportunity to practice lower-level decoding skills and a small number of sight words. Finally, teachers use authentic text (both narrative and nonfiction) to help more advanced readers develop fluency with self-confirmation of accuracy and ease of understanding. In the case of comprehension instruction, we can also utilize listening-level text to develop the language processing abilities that underpin all of the comprehension big ideas—text structure, background knowledge, text cohesion, inference, and the reading/writing connection. Typically used in the form of read-alouds, listening-level text makes it possible for students to build knowledge, vocabulary and other comprehension strategies using text that is more complex and challenging than what students can read themselves.

## Text Selection Skill Analyses

The instructional process involves both explicit content and skill instruction, as well as opportunities to apply those skills in text. This requires teachers to choose text that is best suited to instructional objectives, as well as to analyze how to use it effectively to address the needs of their students. This analytic process involves identifying possible skills within the domain suited to a particular text, and then tailoring language processing activities based on the text. Through this process, any text selection provides an opportunity for teachers to promote text comprehension.

## Now What?

The Literacy How Professional Learning Series is organized for the busy educator who may be trying to find specific information, as well as for the professional seeking deeper understanding of literacy instruction and learning. You can decide which component of the Literacy How Reading Wheel matches your current purpose/interest. In this case, you have selected *Comprehension: Knowledge to Practice* as your area of interest. You will find the information about comprehension divided into Relevant Research, Knowledge for Effective Instruction, Activities for Instruction and Informal Assessment, Text Analyses for Comprehension, and an Appendix. You may wish only to delve into research or you may have a greater need for the activities. It's up to you!

**RELEVANT RESEARCH in Comprehension**

## What is it?

In 1986, Gough and Tunmer proposed the Simple View of Reading (SVR), the idea that reading comprehension is the product of two different skills—**Decoding** and **Comprehension** (see Figure 1). Thirty years of research support this view as the two components explain almost all of the variance in skilled reading comprehension. Decoding, the skill of figuring out unfamiliar words based on knowledge of the alphabetic principle, is required to access the words on the page. Gough and Tunmer used the term *linguistic comprehension* to refer to the process of interpreting words, sentences, and discourse. Since then, countless researchers have studied the SVR and many educators refer to the formula to explain reading. While the term *Decoding* has been used consistently by researchers and practitioners alike, many different terms have been used for *Comprehension* – including *linguistic comprehension, language comprehension,* and *listening comprehension.*

$$R = D \times C$$

Figure 1

Hogan et al. (2011) expanded the SVR by delineating other components of language that contribute to each skill. (See Figure 2.) This expanded view explains that listening comprehension and reading comprehension, though related, are not the same thing. While "reading and listening comprehension draw on many of the same language and cognitive skills" (Hoover & Gough, 1990), reading comprehension is also dependent on fluent word recognition skills. (See *Phonics: Knowledge to Practice* in the Literacy How Professional Learning Series for in depth exploration of this component of reading.)

Figure 2

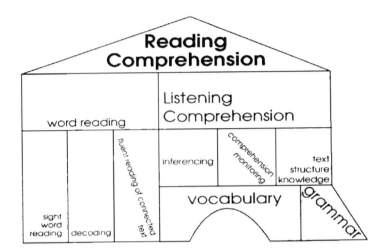

**Figure 1.** Visual representation of the Simple View of Reading including direct and indirect links to reading comprehension through word reading and listening comprehension.

(Hogan, Bridges, Justice, & Cain, 2011)

Castles et al's 2018 article summarizes an important point from the work of the Language and Reading Research Consortium in 2015 – "As children get older, the correlation between linguistic and reading comprehension strengthens, reflecting the fact that once a level of decoding mastery is achieved, reading comprehension is constrained by how well an individual understands spoken language." While children are developing their word recognition skills in the early grades, teachers must build language comprehension through interactive read-alouds and dialogic reading. Listening comprehension, also referred to by some researchers as language comprehension, builds upon the individual's knowledge of vocabulary and syntax. (See *Vocabulary: Knowledge to Practice* and *Syntax: Knowledge to Practice* in the **Literacy How** Professional Learning Series for in depth exploration of these two domains.) In addition to these foundational skills, listening comprehension depends upon students' abilities to make inferences, to connect new information to background knowledge, and to apply their knowledge of text structure.

Students must possess the various language skills described above in order to monitor their comprehension while reading, which in turn requires them to apply a variety of language processing skills (e.g., predicting, clarifying, questioning, and summarizing). This is what we refer to as being metacognitive, that is thinking about what we're reading while we're reading.

Reading comprehension, however, is more than a collection of skills and strategies that students apply to text. The Rand Report (2003) synthesized all the comprehension research to that date. It highlighted the multidimensional nature of reading comprehension that varies as a function of the *reader's* ability, the *text* the student reads, and the *tasks* a teacher asks students to perform as they engage with text. In 2017, Kamhi and Catts revisited the Rand Report to reiterate the multidimensional nature of comprehension and the instructional implications related to its complexity. "The variability of comprehension means that instruction will be more effective when tailored to students' abilities with specific texts and tasks. This instruction would involve identifying educationally relevant reading comprehension activities and directly addressing the component skills and knowledge bases involved in these activities."

## Big Ideas That Shape Comprehension Instruction

Five big ideas shaped our focus for reading comprehension instruction: text structure, background knowledge, coherence, inference, and the reading/writing connection.

**Text Structure:** Text structure refers to how the text's organization guides the reader's comprehension. To understand written text, one must be able to recognize relationships among elements in text (Graesser & Clark, 1985; Langston & Trabasso, 1998). When readers recognize relationships across both sentences and larger units of text, they can form a mental model of what they have read. Researchers have suggested that increasing students' knowledge of text structure facilitates their ability to attend to the most salient details in the text, therefore increasing comprehension (e.g., Carnine & Kinder, 1985; Gersten, Fuchs, Williams, & Baker, 2001).

**Background Knowledge:** Understanding what we read involves not so much the acquisition of new knowledge as it does the modification of knowledge we already have (McNamara & Kintsch, 1996). A reader's background knowledge affects how his attention is directed, how incoming information is interpreted, how it is stored in memory, and the ease with which it can be made available from memory. "Reading is not content free; readers read about something, and the content of that something makes a big difference in how well it is understood" (Beck & McKeown, 2002).

**Coherence**: Skilled readers strive to build coherence in order to understand what a text is trying to communicate (Beck & McKeown, 1981, 1986). As mentioned earlier, proficient readers monitor their comprehension and use metacognitive strategies to build coherence. Specifically, reading comprehension requires the reader "to integrate meaning across sentences" (Cain, 2009). Cohesion represents a convergence of syntactic knowledge and meaning making. Syntax is how certain words link meaning from word to word and sentence to sentence (Schleppegrell, 2013). "The interpretation and use of connectives when reading is crucial to the construction of a coherent situation model of a text, the hallmark of successful comprehension" (Cain & Nash, 2011).

**Inference**: Inference requires the reader "to combine information in the text with general knowledge for inference generation" (Cain, 2009). Readers look for clues to support meaning and fill in the missing details to support their mental model of what the text means. "Less skilled comprehenders may be poorer at knowing when and how to relate general knowledge to the text in order to supply the missing details" (Cain & Oakhill, 2009).

**Reading/writing connection**: Reading and writing share a reciprocal relationship and as such, students benefit from writing about what they read. Teaching writing has a positive impact on reading fluency and reading comprehension (Graham & Hebert, 2010, 2011). In their meta-analysis *Writing to Read* (2010), they found that "students' reading comprehension is improved by having them increase how often they produce their own text." The National Commission on Writing concluded that "if students are to make knowledge their own, they must struggle with the details, wrestle with the facts, and rework raw information and dimly understood concepts into language they can communicate to someone else. In short, if students are to learn, they must write" (2006). Additionally, Hochman and Wexler (2017) describe writing as a window on students' level of understanding. In making the connection between writing and knowledge acquisition, they explain "When students write, they—and their teachers—figure out what they don't understand and what further information they need."

## Language processing versus comprehension strategies

Notably absent from the big ideas delineated above are comprehension strategies. Why? Mounting evidence from cognitive scientists and educational researchers suggests that readers need to understand the text before they are able to determine which strategy to use and how to apply it to support comprehension (Elleman & Compton, 2017; Wexler, 2019; Willingham, 2006). While researchers recommend some attention to strategy instruction, they view its value as contingent upon students understanding text in the first place. Strategy instruction should not supplant instructional time devoted to systematically building content knowledge. Explicit comprehension instruction, as illustrated in this book, will teach students how to process the complex language that they listen to and/or read.

## The Relationship of Executive Functions to Comprehension Monitoring

Reading comprehension is also impacted by the reader's higher order thinking skills, referred to as executive skills or executive functions. These cognitive processes are required to regulate one's thinking in order to accomplish the goal of comprehending what is read. Cartwright (2015) identified processes typically included in the umbrella of executive skills that support reading comprehension – cognitive flexibility, inhibition, monitoring, organization, planning, social understanding, switching or shifting, and working memory. A new line of research is studying the role that executive skills play in children's reading comprehension. It is no surprise that these studies have demonstrated that students who have reading comprehension difficulties, despite adequate decoding skills, have lower levels of executive skills than their peers with stronger comprehension (Cartwright, 2012, 2015).

Comprehension monitoring also involves the capacity to reflect on one's own comprehension and includes the ability to detect inconsistencies within a text. It is important to note that a failure of comprehension or of detection of inconsistencies may in fact stem from lack of general knowledge rather than a failure to monitor comprehension. Good readers are typically aware of their comprehension as they read or listen to written text, and, when they experience difficulty, they automatically use a variety of strategies, such as rereading, to increase their comprehension (Pressley & Afflerbach, 1995); however, young children and those who struggle to comprehend are likely to have difficultly monitoring their comprehension independently because it requires significant cognitive resources, such as memory and attention.

Within each of the big ideas is a dimension of comprehending that builds the reader's capacity to reflect on the degree to which they understand the text. For example, awareness of text structure leads readers to think about the way the parts of the text relate to each other whether a narrative or an informational selection (See Knowledge for Effective Instruction – Text Structure pages 14 – 24, and Developing Narrative Knowledge pages 110 – 124, and Building Background Knowledge pages 125 – 138). Also, attention to connectives, such as pronouns and conjunctions, a dimension of text cohesion, contributes to the reader's understanding of what a text is trying to communicate (See Knowledge for Effective Instruction – Text Cohesion pages 30 – 36, and Text Links pages 139 – 145). Collectively, these abilities help readers build and monitor their comprehension of what they are reading. Let's take a look at what we know from research on **comprehension** in relation to each stage.

| | Developmental Sequence | | |
| --- | --- | --- | --- |
| | **Stage 0** | **Stage 1** | **Stage 2** |
| *Focus of literacy development* | Pre-alphabetic principle; letter naming | Alphabetic principle Decoding and encoding | Orthographic and morphologic patterns |
| *What do we know from research?* | • Comprehension skills develop along with basic language skills and have their roots in early narrative comprehension (Cain & Oakhill, 2007).<br>• Narrative discourse skills predict later reading achievement and academic success (Cain & Oakhill, 2007).<br>• "The goal of invoking background knowledge is to integrate it with content in order to | • "To help children gain success with reading, it is necessary to focus on comprehension early in their experiences. Much of this interaction can and should be done orally; it can't wait for children's word skills to catch up with their conceptual skills" (Beck & McKeown, 2002).<br>• Teachers' open questions elicit greater language production and encourage children to consider important ideas in the story. (Beck & McKeown, 2001).<br>• Text structure can be taught to students and this | • "Text comprehension is a dynamic and interactive process involving several sources of information and knowledge" (Cain, 2009).<br>• Reading informational texts serves several important functions for young readers including building content knowledge and vocabulary, capitalizing on students' interests, presenting opportunities for students to develop areas of expertise, and preparing students for the types of text that they will read most frequently as adults (Duke, 2016). |

| | Developmental Sequence | |
|---|---|---|
| **Stage 0** | **Stage 1** | **Stage 2** |
| assist comprehension… When background knowledge is drawn out, the teacher scaffolds children's responses to make clear the relationship of background knowledge to text ideas" (Beck & McKeown, 2001).<br><br>• "Reading aloud and discussing what is read is an important avenue for helping children deal with decontextualized language" (Beck & McKeown, 2001).<br><br>• "Storybook reading and narrative text may provide even young children with a rich context for developing an understanding of mind" (Dyer et. al., 2000). | awareness can improve reading comprehension (Carlisle & Rice, 2002). Teaching students the structure and sequence in stories can reduce the load on working memory (Westby, 1999).<br><br>• "There is evidence that developing awareness of text structures plays an important role in understanding and remembering texts" (Catts, & Kamhi, 1999).<br><br>• The ability to recognize informational text structures can be developed through the use of signal words, physical features, and graphic organizers (Williams, 2005; Stafford & Williams, 2005). | • "Students who are good comprehenders read for a purpose and actively monitor whether that purpose is being met. They notice when something they are reading is incongruous with their background knowledge or is unclear, then they take action to clarify their understanding such as rereading or reading ahead" (Rand Report, 2002).<br><br>• "… tasks and texts that engage children's interests have been shown to improve performance on higher level comprehension tasks, such as comprehension monitoring, as compared to more traditional drill and skill exercises" (Hogan et. al., 2011).<br><br>• Children who are poor comprehenders benefit from explicit instruction in making inferences (Yuill & Oakhill, 1988).<br><br>• Readers generate inferences while they comprehend narrative text by constructing "rich situation models during the comprehension of narrative" (Graesser, et. al., 1994). |

## English Learners:

- One major theme in the Institute of Education Sciences 2007 Practice Guide (Effective Literacy and English Language Instruction for English Learners in the Elementary Grades) is "the importance of intensive, interactive English language development instruction for all English learners. This instruction needs to focus on developing academic language (the decontextualized language of the schools, the language of academic discourse, of texts, of formal argument). This area, which researchers and practitioners feel has been neglected, is one of the key targets in this Guide."

- Don't assume that all children come with the same knowledge of story structure. When teaching narrative text structure, teachers should keep in mind that the storytelling form differs from culture to culture (McCabe, 1997).

- Help fill in gaps in background knowledge. English Learners (ELs) often have different experiences than other students and may lack background knowledge that is key for inferencing. One effective method for building knowledge is to teach thematic units and the vocabulary associated with the themes.

- An effective technique for ELs is to 'teach the text backwards.' This means that the teacher might begin with an activity related to the theme (e.g., watch a movie or take a field trip), then ask questions to facilitate a discussion about the theme, and *then* read the text.
- ELs who can read in their native language should be given the text/novel to read in that language before beginning the unit.

## Students with Dyslexia/Reading Disabilities

- Dyslexia is primarily a decoding difficulty; however, many children also experience reading comprehension problems associated with co-occurring language difficulties (Hulme & Snowling, 2016).
- "It is possible for a child to have learning differences that impede the development of word recognition and spelling and also to have language impairments that impede the development of comprehension" (Odegard, 2019).
- Although many studies confirm that weak phonological skills are a primary risk factor for poor reading, dyslexia is more likely to be diagnosed when students have difficulties with other language processing abilities, including difficulties with grammar and vocabulary (Hulme & Snowling, 2016).
- There is evidence from intervention studies that language interventions can improve language weaknesses that are detected in the early school years (Hulme & Snowling, 2016).
- Although most students with dyslexia do not have core weaknesses in higher levels of literacy, such as vocabulary, text comprehension, and broad language aspects of written expression, their weaknesses in phonological skills, decoding, and spelling often have secondary negative effects on these higher-level areas (Spear-Swerling, 2018).

**Knowledge for Effective Instruction**

When readers comprehend text, they draw upon the complex oral language system that maps the sounds of language to meaning. This system—comprised of phonological (sound), semantic (meaning), and syntactic (word arrangement) components—provides the foundation to negotiate written language for reading and writing. This chapter explores how comprehending text builds upon these language components and five research-based big ideas.

## The Development of Comprehension Across the Stages

As she did for other aspects of reading development, Chall mapped out changes that occur in language comprehension at each stage. The following table summarizes the key shifts—from oral language comprehension to reading comprehension—that occur across Stages 0 to 2.

| Stage 0<br>Birth to age 6 | Stage 1<br>Grades 1 – 2; ages 6 – 7 | Stage 2<br>Grades 2 – 3; ages 7 – 8 |
|---|---|---|
| • Accumulate fund of knowledge about letters, words, and books<br>• Grow in control of syntax and words<br>• Retell familiar story in a book with aid of pictures (pseudo-reading) | • Move from pseudo-reading to actual/accurate print-to-speech | • Use redundancies of stories (i.e., story structure)<br>• Read a lot of material "that is familiar in its use of language and content." (Chall, page 19). This includes familiar stories, familiar subjects, familiar structures. |
| Before students acquire the alphabetic principle, they largely focus on meaning via listening and speaking the language (i.e., oral language development) | During Stage 1, the focus is on acquiring mastery of the code. Prior "comprehension," acquired through listening and viewing, helps develop fluency. | Identifying words not taught is necessary for proficiency in Stage 2 |

Chall (1967) stressed that a major purpose of reading instruction in Stages 0, 1 and 2 is to move children from learning orally to learning through print. These first three stages prepare for Stage 3 where the shift from "learning to read" to "reading to learn" (i.e., acquisition of new ideas and information from one's own reading) can occur. This shift informs our thinking about instructional emphases to develop comprehension. (See *Competing priorities—mastering decoding vs. developing knowledge* page 27 for more on Chall's position on comprehension.)

## Using the Expanded View of Reading to Inform What to Teach to Develop Comprehension

The expanded view of reading, described in Relevant Research in Comprehension (See pages 5 – 6), provides a blueprint for the areas of knowledge that are needed for effective comprehension instruction. Let's take a look at the relationship between several key areas—word reading, vocabulary, and syntax—and comprehension.

*The relationship between word reading and comprehension*

In order to comprehend what is read, the reader must be able to decode every word accurately and automatically. When readers are inaccurate and/or slow to decode the words in a text, their cognitive energy is consumed as they try to 'lift the words' off the page. In other words, they have limited bandwidth to think about what they're reading – the goal of reading comprehension. As Perfetti (2007) states, "Comprehension depends on successful word reading. Skill differences in comprehension can arise from skill differences in word reading."

Early reading instruction, especially during Stages 1 and 2, must target accurate and automatic word recognition (i.e., reading fluency). Then, when students must *read to learn*, they can focus their cognitive energy on comprehending complex information and ideas so they can build mental models of what they read. (See *Phonemic Awareness and Phonics: Knowledge to Practice* for more information about developing accurate and automatic word recognition ability.)

*The relationship between vocabulary and comprehension*

Vocabulary is the foundation to learn and remember what one is reading (Oakhill & Cain, 2016). To a large extent, vocabulary is a proxy for background knowledge, particularly in content areas (Willingham, 2006; Hirsch, 2003; and Neuman, 2019). Additionally, some types of vocabulary, such as transition words and phrases within the category of academic vocabulary, serve as a tool to navigate genre, text structures, and text cohesion.

Vocabulary instruction should stress the development of deeper meaning/connections and provide repeated exposure to the same words across multiple texts (Oakhill & Cain, 2016). Strategies to use the context and morphological elements contribute to students' ability to figure out the meanings of unfamiliar words. (See *Vocabulary: Knowledge to Practice* for more information.)

*The relationship between syntax and comprehension*

In Cheryl Scott's paper, *A Case for the Sentence in Reading Comprehension* (2009), she states: "If a reader cannot parse the types of complex sentences that are often encountered in academic texts, no amount of comprehension strategy instruction will help." Many syntactic activities develop comprehension skills at the sentence level. This is what Cain (2009) refers to as local coherence.

A useful way to look at grammatical elements, also referred to as parts of speech, is to understand how they serve as the building blocks of comprehension. For example, the words that name people, places and things (i.e., nouns) in our language, serve that same purpose in text. In narrative text, nouns identify characters—the people, animals or imaginary characters that act out the action in the story. In informational text, nouns convey the subject or topic that the text is about. Therefore, a student's syntactic awareness and grammatical ability to identify words based on their function (i.e., the role they play) can facilitate comprehension. The following table summarizes these relationships.

| Functional Grammar* | Informational Text | Narrative Text |
|---|---|---|
| Who/what <br> • Noun <br> • Pronoun | Identify subject/topic | Identify characters |
| Did what? | | Provide actions that drive the plot |
| Adverbs and adverbial structures | Signal text cohesion | Provide elements of setting—time (where) and place (where) |
| Adjectives and adjectival structures | Provide details and examples | Provide character descriptions, traits |
| Meaning links <br> • Pronouns <br> • Prepositions <br> • Conjunctions | Signal topic through referential chains <br> Signal text cohesion <br> Signal text cohesion | Refer to characters |

* For syntax instructional activities, see *Syntax: Knowledge to Practice.*

As summarized here, word reading, vocabulary and syntactic knowledge—individually and interactively—contribute to reading comprehension. Each key area has a unique relationship to comprehension but there is overlap between and among the areas associated with skilled reading.

## Ideas Shaping Comprehension Instruction

The five big ideas outlined in Relevant Research (See pages 7 – 8) – text structure, background knowledge, coherence, inference, and the reading/writing connection—shape the instructional activities we have designed to develop reading comprehension. Indeed, the "big ideas" are interrelated but as with other aspects of explicit instruction, it is helpful to separate the inseparable to consider how best to deliver targeted instruction. Let's take a closer look at the knowledge needed for each of these big ideas.

## Text Structure

Text genre and text structure are often used interchangeably, but they are not the same (Duke, 2014). Text genre speaks to the purpose of the text. The narrative genre conveys a story, while expository text conveys information. Text structure, on the other hand, refers to how an author organizes his text. Both are important in terms of instruction.

Recognizing text structure is useful, because readers who can recognize a text's structure and use it to help organize the information in the text are better comprehenders. As such, teaching text structures supports students' ability to comprehend what they read (Williams, 2003).

## Narrative Text

Narrative text refers to any text that tells a story, including fairy tales, personal narratives, and historical fiction. All narratives have what is referred to as a 'story grammar,' that is, a set of rules or components that organize a well-constructed story. Elements of story grammar include characters, settings, series of events, and a resolution. Narrative text is easier to comprehend than expository text because stories conform to the pattern set forth in the grammar.

### Elements of story structure

Drymock (2007) points out, "Story grammars are rather like the set of grammatical rules that are used to structure sentences." Similar to the finite set of grammatical elements from which we build an infinite number of sentences, the elements of story grammar allow us to create an infinite number of narratives (i.e., stories). Whether the narrative is imaginary (i.e., fictional), personal (i.e., based on a real personal experience), or historical (i.e., the recounting of an historical event), the same elements create the story.

What are the elements of story grammar? The following table provides a brief overview:

### Story Grammar Elements

| Conventional term | Role in story | Fiction | Personal Narrative | Historical Narrative |
|---|---|---|---|---|
| Setting | Tells the time (when) and place (where) the narrative takes place | Once upon a time in a deep, dark forest... | My house An early morning in September | April 15, 1912 North Atlantic Ocean |
| Characters | Tells the people, animals or creatures (who/what) act out the events/reactions | The Three Bears and Goldilocks Main character: Goldilocks | Me, a first grader | Passengers and crew on British Ocean Liner, the Titanic |
| Initiating event | The action or event that sets the story in motion | Goldilocks smells the porridge cooling on the windowsill. | First day of school in a new school | Set off on April 10th for first transatlantic trip |
| Internal Response | The character's feelings about what happened | She feels hungry and is a curious child. | I am excited and nervous at the same time. I look forward to meeting my new classmates. | Excitement because the Titanic was the fastest and thought-to-be safest ship ever built |

| Conventional term | Role in story | Fiction | Personal Narrative | Historical Narrative |
|---|---|---|---|---|
| Plan Attempts, includes climax | What the character plans to do to achieve his/her goals. The sequence of actions the character does to carry out the plan, which includes the climax. | She follows her nose and decides to eat the porridge that she finds in the kitchen. One thing leads to another and she falls asleep in baby bear's bed. | I pack my backpack with my new school supplies and my morning snack. Mommy helps me read the name of my new teacher – Mrs. Baker. I wait for the bus with mommy. | Left England, picked up passengers in France and Ireland before setting off across the ocean. Hit iceberg, which ruptured compartments |
| Consequence/ Resolution | What happens as a result of the plan and attempts. How the character feels about the consequence | She satisfies her curiosity (and her appetite) but the bears find their porridge gone, chairs and beds broken and Goldilocks asleep in their bed. Goldilocks is shocked when she wakes up. She feels some remorse. | I have a great day at school and see two friends from my old school. Mrs. Baker is very nice and I don't feel nervous anymore. I listened to a book about dogs and I look forward to going back to school tomorrow. | Compartments filled with water, ship tilted and sank. Some rescued and taken to Halifax. Many passengers lost at sea. |

These story grammar elements are labeled in different ways within various programs. Despite variation in terminology, stories require these basic elements. "Story grammar research moves the teacher away from general explanations of story structure (e.g., that stories have a beginning, middle and end) to the more specific (e.g., that stories have characters, a theme, and a plot) (Drymock, 2007)." The more specific story grammar elements provide a scaffold that facilitates both understanding and recall. Instruction can merge these two components—story grammar and beginning, middle and end—by emphasizing which story elements typically occur at each point in the story. For example, the characters, setting, initiating event, internal response and plan usually emerge in the beginning; attempts make up the middle of the story; consequences and reaction/resolution occur at the end.

*Features of narrative text*

The purpose of narrative text is to tell a story. To do this, narratives are characterized by particular language signal words, language structures, and cues for comprehension. These features are captured in the following table.

| Type of Text Structure and Function | Language Cue Words (signal words) | Language Structures | Comprehension Cues | Visual Organizer |
|---|---|---|---|---|
| **Narrative** <br> To tell a story | first <br> next <br> then <br> after that <br> finally <br> but <br> so <br> or <br> because <br> if | Simple to complex sentence structures <br><br> Elaborated noun phrases (noun + adjective(s)) <br><br> Adverbs | Where and when does the story take place? <br> Who are the main characters? <br> What thoughts or feelings does the main character have about the problem? | Story = Setting + Episodic Structure |

| Type of Text Structure and Function | Language Cue Words (signal words) | Language Structures | Comprehension Cues | Visual Organizer |
|---|---|---|---|---|
| | since<br>however | Conjunctions; coordinating and subordinating<br><br>Mental verbs:<br>thinking (e.g., think, know, remember, decide)<br>feeling (e.g., hope, worry, care)<br><br>Linguistic verbs (e.g., yelled, said, exclaimed) | What is the main character's goal or plan?<br>What does the character do to carry out the plan?<br>What happens? Is it successful or not?<br>Was that the character's intention?<br>How does the character feel about what happened? | <br><br>See Developing Narrative Knowledge pp. 112 – 126. |

Literacy How, 2008, Adapted from M. Moreau

*The dynamics that drive a narrative*

Moreau provides a student-friendly model—the Critical Thinking Triangle—to support students in their understanding of the dynamics that drive a narrative. Utilizing a visual (see below), the model is designed to capture "the inferred emotions and thinking that occur" after an initiating event and to help students master the language needed to express the dynamics of a story (Moreau, 2016).

The Critical Thinking Triangle (CTT) incorporates three important elements of story grammar – the initiating event, the internal responses or feelings, and the plan for action. (See Figure 3.) It also includes two additional elements: 1) mental state or thinking verbs and 2) cohesive words that connect the three components of the triangle. Mental state verbs (e.g., think, know, remember) are important, because they provide the language to demonstrate students' understanding of how characters have different perspectives. This language processing can be facilitated through the use of sentence frames (e.g., I think that_____. I feel that _____.) Furthermore, as Moreau states, "perspective taking is a high-level language task which combines content and sentence structure." Cohesive words, referred to as conjunctions in Moreau's model, allow students to use complex sentence structures to show relationships, make inferences, and connect ideas. For example, the use of "but" can show a change in direction (e.g., The temperature dropped sharply below freezing, **but** the parrots survived the cold.) and the use of "because" signals a reason (e.g., They were concerned for the parrots, **because** the temperature fell below freezing.) The teacher can use the five parts of the CTT to explicitly teach students to express orally their understanding of stories that they read or listen to.

Figure 3

## 5 Elements of The Critical Thinking Triangle®

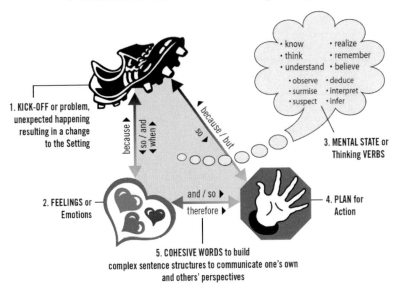

Used with permission: Moreau, 2016

**Critical Thinking Triangle**

*Stages of narrative development*

Children learn about narrative through various stages of development. Westby and Culatta (2016) have provided us with a developmental sequence of narrative development. The following table relates narrative development to Chall's stages of reading development to help inform expectations for students' level of narrative knowledge across these stages. This table demonstrates that children's ability to understand the elements of a story develops sequentially and as such, teachers must differentiate their instruction based on where students are on this developmental continuum.

## Chall's Stages of Reading Development

| Stage 0 | Stage 1 | Stage 2 |
|---|---|---|
| Grades: Pre – K<br>Ages: 3 – 5 | Grades: K – 2<br>Ages: 5 – 7 | Grades: 2 – 3<br>Ages: 7 – 9 |

Stages of Narrative Development

**Descriptive sequence** is a series of sentences with character(s) and/or where they are

**Action Sequence** is a series of actions that include a connective (e.g., and, first, then). The story may include a character(s) and where they are.

**Reactive Sequence** is a story with a chain of actions that includes a cause-effect sentence(s).

**Abbreviated Episode** is a story with a chain of actions that includes an initiating event (i.e., problem), an internal response (i.e., character's reaction/feelings), and consequences.

**Complete Episode** is a chain of actions that includes an initiating event (i.e., problem), an integral response (i.e., character's reaction/feelings) plan, attempts to carry out the plan, and consequences.

**Complex Episode** is a story with all of the elements of a complete episode but with obstacles and several attempts to carry out the plan.

*Why narrative text is easier*

Teachers often gravitate toward the use of narrative text in the primary grades. Why this tendency? In general, narrative text is easier to comprehend. The table below contrasts features of narrative and expository texts to show ways in which narrative text is easier.

| Features | Narrative | Expository |
|---|---|---|
| Text Structure | One structure: Story Grammar | Several structures: Description, Sequence, Problem-Solution, Compare-Contract, Cause-Effect<br><br>Several structures may be present in one book |
| Sentence Structure | Simple, compound, and complex sentences<br><br>Use of dialogue | Short simple sentences |
| Cohesive Ties | Temporal ties (first, then, next, finally)<br>Additive<br>Adversative (but, so) | Text for early readers has simple text structure so it lacks cohesive ties that are present in compound and complex sentences (e.g., temporal, additive) |
| Other Cohesive Devices | | Referential ties (pronoun referents, use of synonyms) |
| Vocabulary/Background Knowledge | | Use of novel/new vocabulary that is content-based |

Now let's contrast narrative structure with expository text structures with an eye to their relative difficulty and the instruction implications.

## Expository Text

*A foundational structure*

Expository text, also referred to as informational text, has a variety of organizational structures depending on what type of information is being conveyed and the relationship of that information within the text. The most basic relationship—main ideas and supporting details—is a hierarchical one. Main ideas and supporting details answer two key questions: *Who or what is the text about?* and *What does this tell about the main idea?*. The following graphic illustrates the supporting role of the details to the main idea.

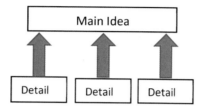

Let's look at an example. In the following passage about marine iguanas, students need to identify the main idea as marine iguanas and how and why they move. Details in the passage support the reasons marine iguanas move (Hughes, 2013). The graphic illustrates this relationship.

Marine iguanas swim well. Their long tails swoosh from side to side, pushing them through the water.

The iguanas dive to eat algae that grow on rock underwater. The iguanas cling to the rocks using their long claws. They scrape the algae off the rocks with their sharp teeth.

Marine iguanas get cold swimming in the ocean. They come ashore to warm themselves in the sun.

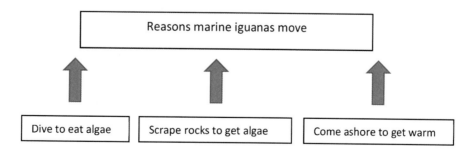

*Features of informational text structures*

Although a main idea with its supporting details is the foundational structure of informational text, to limit expository text structure analysis to this single relationship is to miss both the complexity and power of other informational text structures. In addition to this basic structure, there are at least five different expository structures as displayed in the table below. Each type of text structure is characterized by its function, the language signal words that are commonly used, language structures, cues for comprehension, and a graphic organizer used as a visual representation for the particular structure. Recognizing a text's structure and using it to organize and retrieve information are important skills for comprehending and remembering the information in the text. Conversely, students who have difficulty doing this, may have greater difficulty understanding and recalling what they read in informational text.

| Type of Text Structure and Function | Language Cue Words (signal words) | Language Structures | Comprehension Cues | Visual Organizer |
|---|---|---|---|---|
| **Descriptive**<br><br>To tell what something is | for example<br>characteristics<br>for instance<br>such as<br>is like<br>including<br>to illustrate<br>for instance<br>also<br>and<br>specifically<br>it means | Simple to complex elaborated noun phrases | Define...<br>Describe...<br>List...<br>What is...<br>Who is... | |
| **Sequence**<br><br>To tell what happened or how to do or make something | first<br>next<br>then<br>second<br>third<br>before<br>finally<br>after<br>now<br>eventually<br>previously<br>actual use of dates | Temporal conjunctions | Give the steps...<br>When did...happen?<br>What is the sequence of events? | 1._____<br>2._____<br>3._____<br>4._____ |

| Type of Text Structure and Function | Language Cue Words (signal words) | Language Structures | Comprehension Cues | Visual Organizer |
|---|---|---|---|---|
| **Problem and Solution**<br><br>To state a problem and offer solutions | the problem is<br>a solution is<br>if/then<br>because<br>so that<br>question/answer<br>as a result<br>therefore<br>consequently<br>solve | Adverbial clauses | Describe the problem of...<br>What are some possible solutions to...? | Problem → Solution |
| **Cause and Effect**<br><br>To explain or give reasons why something happens or exists | if/then<br>cause/reason<br>reasons why<br>as a result<br>results or effects<br>therefore<br>because<br>consequently<br>since<br>so<br>for this reason<br>in order to<br>affects<br>hence<br>due to<br>thus<br>leads to | Causal conjunctions connecting two ideas in a sentence are a signal that there is a causal coherence relation. | Explain...<br>Predict...<br>Why did...happen?<br>How did ... happen?<br>Give the causes (reasons, effects, results, etc.) of... | Cause — Effect / Effect / Effect |
| **Comparison/ Contrast**<br><br>To show likenesses and differences | however<br>different<br>still<br>rather than<br>instead of<br>nevertheless<br>on the other hand<br>but<br>similarly<br>although<br>also<br>in contrast/comparison<br>alike<br>both<br>all<br>same as<br>or<br>in the same way<br>just like<br>yet    unlike | Adversative conjunctions signal that a clause has information that is different from the main clause. | Compare and contrast...<br>How are ...alike and different? | (Venn diagram) |

Literacy How, 2008, Adapted from R. Paul, 2007

Contributing further to the relative difficulty in reading informational text is the fact that frequently, informational text selections combine several of these types of text structures in one selection. For example, an informational selection about plants might begin with a descriptive text structure that provides characteristics of plants. The selection might continue with a sequence structure telling how a plant develops from a seed to a mature plant. Another type of text structure might compare the types of plants that thrive in a dry climate with those that do well in a wet climate. Within this single selection, three types of text structures—descriptive, sequence, and compare/contrast—are used to convey information about plants. And, each type of text requires a recognition of different features to recall information.

While knowledge of the multiple types of informational text structures is ultimately important for students to learn, typically a main idea with supporting detail structure is the focus for beginning reading instruction. Each text structure should be taught explicitly using graphic organizers like those in the table of expository text structures (above) as a visual support. Descriptive and sequence structures are the easiest ones to teach because they are similar to narrative structure where the characters and setting are being **_described_** and the plan and attempts are a **_sequence_** of events.

*Using text structure to assess comprehension*

Rubrics provide a framework to rate student performance along a continuum of performance-based descriptors to reflect the level of proficiency of a student's retelling. Retelling rubrics can help teachers assess global aspects of students' retelling that are relevant to any type of text. Global rubrics focus on features such as the use of complete sentences, inclusion of key information, and use of passage-specific vocabulary. Ratings on a scale from 1 to 4 for each retelling element provide valuable information to guide instruction. Other rubrics based on the structure of the text—narrative or expository—can provide feedback regarding students' ability to use text structure to recall and state text content. For example, a narrative retelling rubric uses the elements of story grammar as its framework. Teachers can use this rubric to rate students' ability to include information about characters, setting, and outcomes. Similarly, a rubric designed for retelling an expository passage might rate the inclusion of main ideas and relevant supporting details, use of transition words that reflects the organization of the text (e.g., for sequence – first, next, last; cause-effect – if/then, as a result), and the use of topic-specific vocabulary. Used at various points during the school year, ratings on the same rubric can capture changes in student performance. Ratings can also inform instructional focus. Students who omit key elements of story grammar or those who use general vocabulary rather than topic-specific words, will need a different instructional emphasis. (See **Activities for Instruction and Informal Assessment** pages 101 – 104 and **Appendix** pages 186 – 189.)

## Background knowledge

Background knowledge—the fund of information garnered from real life experiences, watching videos, listening to stories and informational text, and eventually reading oneself—is a key factor in the development of fluent word recognition, vocabulary growth, and inference-making. Students accumulate this type of knowledge by listening to informational text and reading deeply as decoding abilities develop.

*Why it's important*

Simply put, background knowledge is important because it is foundational for nearly every component of reading. To help visualize the relationship between background knowledge and the components of reading, we adapted the

Figure 4

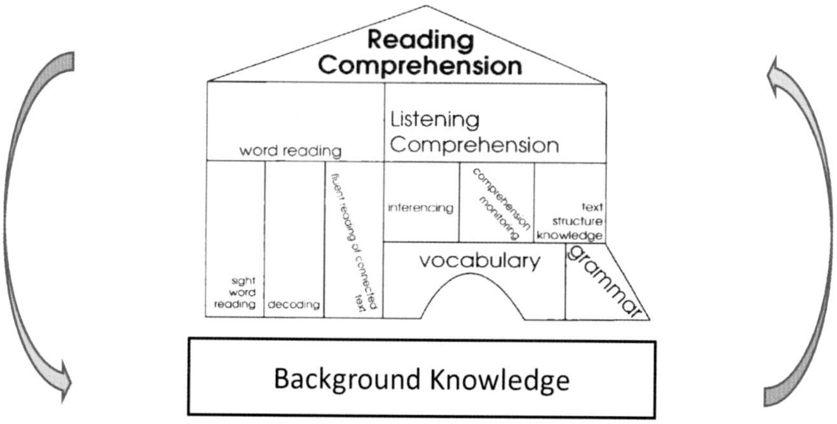

Hogan, Bridges, Justice, & Cain, 2011

expanded view of reading (See **Relevant Research**, page 6) by adding background knowledge as a foundational component below the reading house graphic. (See Figure 4.) The arrows signal the synergistic relationship between background knowledge and reading comprehension: background knowledge is necessary to comprehend; reading adds to background knowledge. Let's explore why and how background knowledge is important to the components of reading, and especially to comprehension.

Evidence from an often-replicated study referred to as "The Baseball Study" reveals that "students who did poorly on a standardized reading test but knew a lot about baseball were better able to comprehend a reading passage than "good" readers who knew little about baseball—when the subject was baseball (Recht & Leslie, 1988)." The researchers found that knowledge of the topic had a much greater impact on comprehension than generalized ability did. "It appears therefore that knowledge of a content domain is a powerful determinant of the amount and quality of information recalled, powerful enough for poor readers to compensate for their generally low reading ability (Recht & Leslie, 1988)." This finding underscores the importance of building students' background knowledge in the quest to ensure good reading comprehension since comprehension <u>depends on background knowledge</u>. As Willingham (2006) says, "knowing the subject makes you a good reader." Additionally, this finding provides the incentive to begin building background knowledge well-ahead of the point when students can read on their own.

Neuman (2019) explains that "vocabulary is children's entry to knowledge and the world of ideas." Content knowledge and vocabulary growth are inextricably linked (Hirsch, 2003). Therefore, another important aspect of building background knowledge is that it simultaneously builds vocabulary knowledge. Additionally, systematic content domain instruction presents students with new vocabulary within a context in which the words are thematically and conceptually related making it easier for the words to "stick." Through a combination of repeated exposures to words, child-friendly definitions, and the development of categorical word networks, children can—and must—build domain knowledge to build vocabulary. (See **Vocabulary: Knowledge to Practice** for more about vocabulary development and instructional practices.)

Hirsch (2003) points out that "fluency is also increased by domain knowledge, which allows the reader to make rapid connections between new and previously learned content; this both eases and deepens comprehension." Similar to the way that rapid and accurate decoding of words frees up working memory and allows the reader to focus on meaning, a student's prior knowledge about a topic frees up working memory and permits the reader to connect prior information to new content and to draw inferences. The more the reader knows about a topic, the faster that individual can take in new information.

Oakhill and Yuill (1996) make a case for focusing on the development of general knowledge due to its significant role in making inferences. Comprehension requires readers to use prior knowledge—both experiential and domain-based—to fill gaps (i.e., make inferences), because writers do not include every detail in the text. Willingham (2006) explains that "comprehension demands background knowledge because language is full of semantic breaks in which knowledge is assumed and, therefore, comprehension depends on making correct inferences." As Oakhill and Yuill (1996) emphasize, a lack of general knowledge is one of the reasons for inferencing difficulties. (See the **Inference** section pages 37 – 45.)

The National Reading Panel (2000) cited reading comprehension as one of the five evidence-based pillars of reading instruction. Unfortunately, in the report's emphasis on reading strategies it "failed to mention the strong evidence showing that the most important factor in comprehension isn't mastering strategies: It's how much knowledge a reader has of the topic" (Wexler, 2019). Wexler points out that all of the comprehension strategies endorsed by the panel "rely on activating prior knowledge—which means they only work if a reader has enough background knowledge to understand the text in the first place." Wexler (2018) cites cognitive scientist Daniel Willingham to further clarify: "whether or not readers understand a text depends far more on how much background knowledge and vocabulary they have relating to the topic than on how much they've practiced comprehension skills." Willingham explains that writers leave out information assuming readers will be able to call upon their background knowledge to fill gaps and make inferences, both of which are critical to comprehending text.

Wexler (2019) also cites the oft-overlooked role of knowledge in the Common Core State Standards. She points out that one of the "three shifts" in emphasis in the standards is that "students must have 'extensive opportunities to build knowledge' through 'content-rich nonfiction.'" The ability for students to accomplish the other two shifts— regular practice reading complex text and the need to be able to ground claims in evidence from the text—are both contingent upon understanding the text in the first place, something that Wexler argues requires knowledge.

*Competing priorities—mastering decoding vs. developing knowledge*

While we have relied on Chall's stages of reading development to frame the evolution of reading abilities, this developmental framework is not intended to dichotomize an instructional focus on decoding versus comprehension. In fact, Chall (1967) warned that there was certainly the potential for reading instruction to tilt too far in the direction of phonics instruction, something that concerned her.

Wexler's recent book, *The Knowledge* Gap, explores how a singular emphasis on decoding has had the unintended negative consequence of limiting the amount of time devoted to instruction that develops background knowledge. As important as decoding is, Wexler's point is that it isn't an "either/or" or "first/then" option—in terms of teaching decoding or focusing on background knowledge—but rather a matter of doing *both*. She makes this point clearly stating, "Teachers who reject phonics surely want their students to learn to appreciate literature, acquire knowledge independently, and love reading. I'm not sure how to convince skeptics that the most effective route to accomplishing those objectives is to teach phonics systematically while building knowledge through read-alouds and discussion" (Wexler, 2019).

Research conducted by McNamara, Ozuru, & Floyd (2011) also provides evidence for the role that knowledge plays in the young reader's ability to comprehend, stating that "decoding skill benefited comprehension, but effects of text genre and cohesion depended less on decoding skill than prior knowledge." This finding provides further rationale for teachers to begin building background knowledge well-ahead of the point when students can read on their own. As Wright (2019) states, "We can't wait for children to decode fluently in order to build their knowledge of the world." Waiting until children can read the content themselves widens the information gap and allows it to grow to a detrimental—even insurmountable—scale . The importance of building students' knowledge early while they are mastering the code cannot be overstated. (See section *The value of read-alouds* pages 60 – 61.)

While there is never enough instructional time in the school day to teach everything a child needs to learn, teachers need to use data to determine what the priorities should be. Since the evidence suggests that all students benefit from more content knowledge, this should be the priority for all students, while ensuring that they can read fluently—that is, accurately, automatically, and with prosody. (See *Phonemic Awareness and Phonics: Knowledge to Practice* for elaboration on the code-breaking skills students require.)

*How to develop background knowledge with beginning readers*

Instructional practices that are cumulative, deliberate, and engaging are key to effectively building background knowledge. Several practices and programs illustrate these principles.

According to Wright (2019), "researchers have shown that reading sets of texts that are conceptually or thematically related can be particularly beneficial for building knowledge." Instructional strategies and programs that incorporate this practice are effective because vocabulary and information are added gradually over time. Wexler says the key is "to not jump from one topic to another, but to read a series of texts on the same general topic" (2019, personal communication). She adds that listening-level nonfiction for beginning readers should include fact-based narratives in science and history to lay the foundation for scientific and historical topics in later grades. The activity **Knowledge Trees** is based on this principle (See pages 125 – 138). "Article-a-Day," available through Read Works [www.readworks.org], also translates this principle into practice. A 10-minute daily routine using sets of articles related by topic are designed to increase students' background knowledge, as well as vocabulary and reading stamina. The natural repetition of content in meaningful contexts has a positive effect on word learning (Wright, 2019). Newsela (www.newsela.com), an online source of informational text, provides the same article written at five different Lexile levels. This resource makes it possible for students reading at different levels to have access to the same information.

Liben and Davidson (2019) provide examples of curricula and programs, such as *Core Knowledge* (Hirsch, 1991), *EL Language Arts* from Open Educational Resources (OER), *Wit & Wisdom* (https://greatminds.org/english), and American Reading Company's *ARC Core*, that are designed to build knowledge and vocabulary cumulatively and systematically from the primary grades through high school. For example, in history, the progression could be Native Americans and Columbus in kindergarten; the colonial era and the American Revolution in first grade; the War of 1812 and the Civil war in second grade, and so on. The following table from the Knowledge Matters website illustrates how knowledge-building might be sequenced in the primary grades.

|  | First Grade | Second Grade | Third Grade |
| --- | --- | --- | --- |
| **World History** | Ancient civilizations in China, Egypt, and the Middle East | Ancient Greece and Rome | Mayans, Aztecs, and Incas |
| **U.S. History** | The 18th century: Native Americans, colonies, and the struggle for independence | The 19th century: Westward expansion and the struggle for freedom | The 20th century: Technological progress, protecting freedom around the world, and the struggle for equality |
| **Arts in U.S. History** | Native American baskets, pottery, and beadwork, and folk art paintings | Songs of liberty (e.g., "Star Spangled Banner"), African American spirituals, and Hudson River School paintings | Modern art, jazz, and the impact of radio and recording on popular music |
| **Life Science** | Common North American habitats: Forests grasslands, wetlands and deserts | Unique North American habitats: The Florida Everglades, Rocky Mountains, and the Mojave Desert | Extreme habitats: Life in the Arctic, the Antarctic, and on the equator |
| **Astronomy** | Earth, sun, and moon | Our solar system | Orbits, rotation and revolution, and the phases of our moon |

Used with permission from Knowledge Matters, www.KnowledgeMattersCampaign.org

This approach enables children to make sense of what they're learning, and the repetition of concepts and vocabulary in different contexts makes it more likely they'll retain the information (Wexler, 2018). In addition to focusing on building knowledge, the implementation of such curricula increases the time spent learning content across a range of subject areas, one of the recommendations of Knowledge Matters, an organization dedicated to resetting schools' focus on building students' knowledge. Knowledge Matters cautions about the negative consequences of narrowing a knowledge-rich curriculum while focusing on code-based instruction in the early grades. They emphasize the long-range importance of building knowledge and vocabulary in the elementary grades.

Finally, project-based instruction, as described by Duke (2014), increases students' use of informational text to complete a project with a real-world purpose for reading and writing. In this approach, the development of a knowledge base results from reading, listening or viewing content to address the goals of the project. In addition to being conceptually related and goal-oriented, knowledge acquired for the project provides a practical application, which in turn adds a layer of motivation and engagement for students.

## Text cohesion

Beck and McKeown (1981, 1986) emphasize the fact that skilled readers strive to build coherence as they read. Though closely related, there is an important distinction between coherence and cohesion. **Coherence** refers to the way text makes sense. To a large extent, coherence is dependent on the reader's ability to make connections between what they are reading (or listening to) and what they already know. For this reason, coherence relies on the reader's background and vocabulary knowledge. **Cohesion** – where grammar and comprehension meet – is what Westby refers to as "reading across text between sentences" (Westby, 2005). Cohesion requires the reader to use grammatical and semantic links (i.e., cohesive ties) within the text to connect meaning across sentences.

The following table delineates this distinction:

| | What is it? | What helps develop it? |
|---|---|---|
| Coherence | The connections between the text and the readers' language and knowledge (i.e., coherence lies in the mind of the reader) | Background knowledge; vocabulary knowledge |
| Cohesion | Cohesion is linking within a text that holds it together and gives it meaning. (i.e., cohesion lies within the text) <br><br> • Relates to the overlap between words, word stems, or concepts from one sentence to another <br> • Relates to "how well the events, ideas, and information of the whole text are tied together." | Understanding the distinction between two types of cohesion and cohesive ties: <br><br> • **Referential cohesion**: synonyms; pronouns (e.g., they, them, their) <br><br> • **Deep cohesion:** Conjunctions; adverbs <br>   • Temporal (e.g., before, after) <br>   • Causal (e.g., because) <br>   • Additive (e.g., furthermore) <br>   • Logical (e.g., as a result) <br>   • Adversative (e.g., however) |

In the following excerpt from *The Wild Parrots of Telegraph Hill* (Bittner, 2004), we provide examples of coherence (blue font) and cohesion (red font and bold).

> *Just before Christmas that year*, an unusual *cold spell* hit The Bay Area.
>
> It rarely freezes in San Francisco, but one night the temperature fell
>
> to twenty-eight degrees. As it grew colder, I started worrying about the **parrots**.
>
> I'd been impressed by **their** tenacity, *but* it seemed to me that an actual freeze
>
> would surely be **their** doom.

The first example, "just before Christmas that year," requires the reader to use prior background knowledge to recognize that the reference to Christmas signals that it is winter when temperatures might be cold. In the second example, "cold spell," requires that the reader knows that the word **spell** can refer to a period of time instead of how to encode words. And specifically, a **cold spell** is a period of cold weather. This background information—the time of year and meaning of cold spell—connects to the concerns for the parrots in the clause "that an actual freeze would surely be their doom" at the end of the paragraph. Both demonstrate how the use of prior knowledge and vocabulary knowledge contributes to the text making sense, and as such, builds coherence.

The other two examples illustrate how text cohesion differs from coherence. The use of the possessive pronoun **their** links the phrases **their tenacity** and **their doom** to the **parrots**. In contrast, the conjunction **but** illustrates how a conjunction can signal a contrast in information within a sentence—the narrator's observation of the parrots' tenacity contrasted with their possible doom. Awareness of and attention to the conjunction—and its impact on meaning—helps the reader build an understanding of the narrator's concern.

*Why text cohesion is important*

"Cohesion is crucial to comprehension, particularly for readers who have low domain knowledge" (Jackson, Allen & McNamara, 2016). According to Graesser, et. al. (2003), "processing coherence relations is a cornerstone of comprehension." Whether using prior knowledge or detecting words that signal text-connecting relations, readers look for clues to support meaning and fill in the missing details to support their mental model of what the text means. Because the goal of comprehending text is to create a mental model of what is read, processing coherence is essential.

Cohesion is also important because it is a key variable in determining text complexity. "There is considerable evidence that cohesion critically determines both how challenging a text is and how well the reader will understand it" (McNamara, Graesser, McCarthy & Cai, 2014). The more writers use cohesive devices, the more they facilitate the across-text associations needed to understand the text. The authors go on to explain that "adding cohesion to the text where needed is presumably facilitative to reading comprehension" and "increasing text cohesion improves readers' understanding and memory for text." Teaching students to recognize and use cohesive ties, therefore, should help them better understand the text.

Mesmer (2017) stresses the importance of anaphora, "a device used in writing in which one word—either a pronoun or another word—replaces another word." She outlines three reasons that teaching anaphora in particular is important. First, an inability to follow the thread of micro-level comprehension conveyed by anaphoric relationships can cause confusion for readers. Next, teachers rarely provide explicit instruction about anaphoric relationships because it is part of limited attention to grammar in United States classrooms. Finally, understanding anaphoric relationships, that is words replacing other words in text, empowers students with metalinguistic awareness about their language, which can facilitate both reading comprehension and writing.

Schleppergrell (2013) advocates explicit instruction in the language that writers use to create cohesion. She explains that this is important because "developing readers often fail to recognize that the same concept or character is being referred to when writers and speakers use a range of linguistic resources, including pronouns and synonyms, to develop cohesive chains of reference. After introducing a concept or character, the author may continue to refer to the same character or concept using a different language form, creating a chain of reference." For readers to fully understand the text, they need to follow the chain of references.

*A closer look at anaphoric relationships and connectives*

Writers use a variety of types of cohesive ties to link together different parts of the text (McNamara, Graesser, McCarthy & Cai, 2014). Cohesive ties fall into two main categories: anaphoric relationships and connectives. Pronouns take their meaning from another point in the text, namely from an antecedent; they link back to nouns that precede them (See *Syntax: Knowledge to Practice* **Meaning Links** for more information.) Other anaphoric relationships are conveyed by synonyms, a word or phrase that means the same thing as another word or phrase. The following table illustrates these two types of anaphoric relationships (Mesmer, 2017).

|  | **Pronoun** | **Synonym Substitution** |
|---|---|---|
| Noun | The parrots' feathers matched the tree's leaves. They were a perfect camouflage. | The parrots climbed tree limbs to get berries. The ripe fruit was a prized goal. |
| Verb |  | One parrot squawked with excitement. The others screamed back. |
| Clause |  | The parrots survived the cold spell, which brought a great sense of relief. It was a comfort to know the freezing temperature wasn't their doom. |

Connectives are words that signal the relationship between words, phrases and sentences. "Connectives consist of many different categories, including temporal (e.g., after), causal (e.g., because), additive (e.g., furthermore), logical (e.g., as a result), and adversative (e.g., however). All of these connectives help to tie together the events, ideas, and information in the text for the reader" (Jackson, Allen & McNamara, 2016). The use of connectives signal these relationships and can facilitate ease of understanding the text. The following sentences illustrate this point.

(A) Smoking was forbidden. The store had inflammables.

(B) Smoking was forbidden **because** the store had inflammables.


"The addition of the cohesive cue "because" in example B is not a compulsory rule of language; nonetheless, its addition facilitates the understanding of *why smoking was forbidden*" (McNamara, Graesser, McCarthy & Cai, 2014).


*Cohesion, text structure, and text complexity*


The difference between anaphoric relationships and connectives underpin the distinction between referential cohesion and deep cohesion, two components of the Coh-Metrix Easability tool (www.CommonCoreTERA.com) designed to analyze text complexity. *Referential cohesion* is "the overlap in words or semantic references, between units in the text such as clauses sentences and paragraphs…. Studies have demonstrated that referential overlap impacts reading times and recall of words and sentences." *Deep cohesion*, on the other hand, refers to the causal, intentional, and temporal connectives that help the reader to form a more coherent and deeper understanding of the text. It pertains to "how well the events, ideas, and information of the whole text are tied together" (McNamara, Graesser, McCarthy & Cai, 2014). In addition to being a component of the Coh-Metrix tool, this distinction between referential and deep cohesion points to aspects of instructional focus to help students navigate complex text. Furthermore, as illustrated by the Coh-Metrix profiles that follow (Figure 5), understanding these types of cohesion provides additional insight about the type of text structure (i.e., narrative versus informational). The types of cohesive devices often differ depending on the text structure as noted in the table on pages 16 – 17 and 22 – 23 in the column labeled Language Cue Words. For example, in the informational excerpt *Parrots*, the referential cohesion score is 50%, where repetition of references to the topic (i.e., parrots) is relatively high. In contrast, in the narrative excerpt *The Wild Parrots of Telegraph Hill*, the referential cohesion score of 18% paired with a high deep cohesion score of 60% and narrativity score of 90%, reflecting the language features characteristic of a story.

## Parrots

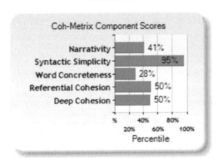

**Flesch-Kincaid Grade Level: 6**

Some parrots are better at imitating than others. Different species mimic for different reasons. For example, African grey parrots in the wild can copy other kinds of birds. Species of Amazon parrots can imitate their own kind.

© Eberhardt &Gillis 2017

## The Wild Parrots of Telegraph Hill

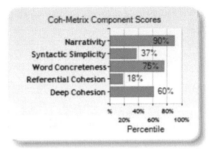

**Flesch-Kincaid Grade Level: 5**

The first time I saw them was on Russian Hill at a housecleaning job. I was on my knees, dusting an end table, when I noticed four brightly colored birds clinging to a small feeder that hung just outside the living room window.

McNamara, Graesser, & Cai (2014)

Figure 5

*Instructional considerations*

As Mesmer (2017) points out, teachers rarely provide sufficient instruction in sentence-level (syntactic) meaning despite the role connectives have in helping readers build an understanding of text. Several types of words in English link meaning within and across sentences.

- **Prepositions** signal the relationship between words.
- **Pronouns** take the place of or refer to a namer (noun).
- **Conjunctions** are a group of words that join words, phrase or clauses
- **Relative pronouns** introduce dependent clauses to signal a relationship to a noun.

Explicit instruction in words that link meaning can foster comprehension. (See *Syntax: Knowledge to Practice* **Meaning Links** activities for effective ways to teach these words.)

Oakhill and Cain (2016) advocate using activities that "show how cohesive devices work and those that contrast the meaning of similar looking sentences." For example, sentences in which the prepositions are different can illustrate how a single word can convey a different meaning. The use of illustrations along with sentences helps reinforce the impact on meaning of these little words and can encourage students to visualize the meaning of the text.

> The ball is **on** the box.
>
> The ball is **under** the box.

Similarly, sentence pairs with different coordinating conjunctions can draw attention to their role in changing meaning.

> Olivia prefers cake **and** ice cream.
>
> Olivia prefers cake **or** ice cream.

The first sentence means that Olivia wants both items, which is signaled by the conjunction **and**. In contrast, the second sentence suggests that Olivia must make a choice, which is signaled by the conjunction **or**.

Schlepppergrell (2013) suggests that taking time to identify and relate the words and phrases through which referential chains are developed helps students gain insight into both the content of what they are reading and how the language resources work." For example:

> **George Washington** served our country in several important ways. **This great man** led the armies to victory. **He** went on to become the first President of the United States.

Knowing that "this great man" in the second sentence refers to George Washington is an example of referential cohesion. In the third sentence "he" also refers to Washington. Understanding both types of referential overlap is essential for surface level comprehension of text. When beginning readers identify these kinds of connections while reading, they are taking the first step in monitoring their own comprehension. (See **Text Links** activity pages 141 – 147.)

Jennings and Haynes (2018) recommend the use of "micro-discourse, short units of text, that is typically two to three sentences, that are related in meaning to develop the ability to recognize and write using referential cohesion". A mnemonic—the Cohesion Circle—guides students' use of synonyms and pronouns in their writing. The same mnemonic helps them track referential words across several sentences to facilitate their reading comprehension. (See Figure 6).

**Strategy:** Teach Cohesion Circle mnemonic.

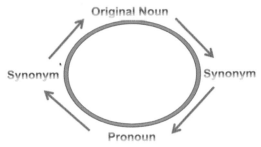

- Jennings & Haynes, 2018

Used with permission from Jennings & Haynes, 2018

Figure 6

One of the major findings in reading comprehension with instructional implications is the distinction between reading processes and products. "Distinguishing between products and processes is important because the two are causally related: Reading processes lead to reading products" (McNamara & Kendeou, 2011). To focus on the process of comprehension, what we do as teachers needs to focus on what the reader is doing *while* reading. One way to accomplish this is through the use of think-aloud strategies. These strategies, which rely on teacher modeling of the thought processes an experienced reader uses, can help students look for and interpret cohesive ties while reading. The following examples from *The Empty Pot* (Demi, 1990) illustrate this process.

| Sentence in the Text | Teacher Think-Aloud |
|---|---|
| A long time ago in China there was a boy named Ping who loved flowers. Anything **he** planted burst into bloom. | Who is **he** referring to? **He** refers to Ping, the boy who loved flowers. |
| The Emperor loved birds and animals, but flowers most of all, and he tended his own garden every day. **But** the Emperor was very old. | The word **but** tells us that we are going to learn something different about the Emperor. |

Through the think-aloud process, teachers can focus on meaning links that are a part of the students' explicit instruction. For instance, if instruction focuses on pronouns, the think-aloud should model the identification of the antecedent for the pronouns. Similarly, if instruction addresses the role of coordinating conjunctions, the think-aloud should verbalize the way in which the conjunction joins words within the sentence.

# Inference

McNamara and Kendeou (2011) explain that, "in the context of reading comprehension, inferencing is the process of connecting information within the text or within the text and one's knowledge base, and drawing a conclusion that is not explicitly stated in the text." Simply put, inference is reading between the lines, or figuring out what's *not* in print. This is in contrast to cohesion, which uses what *is* in print.

*Why it's important*

The ability to make inferences (i.e., gap-fill missing information) is required to understand what we read and is considered a higher-order cognitive skill that contributes to the creation of the reader's mental model. The mental model is constructed as the reader creates representations of the text ideas. Kintsch (1998) refers to this as a 'situation model' and describes it as a "dynamic constructive process that is determined by the interaction of the reader, the text structures, and the semantic content." The situation model includes the reader's representations of what that text means and incorporates connections that we make to our background knowledge. A child's ability to inference supports the construction of the mental or situation model and is essential to the coherence-building process that is central to comprehension.

By grade 4, students at the basic level are expected to make simple inferences on reading assessments such as the National Assessment of Education Progress (NAEP). Students at the proficient and advanced levels, however, are expected to make complex inferences within and across literary and informational texts in order to comprehend. As such, the nation's report card assesses these inferencing skills by expecting students to summarize major ideas, draw conclusions and provide supporting information, and to integrate ideas and find evidence in support of an argument. Furthermore, Marzano (2010) suggests that inference is one of the foundational processes upon which a number of the necessary 21st century skills, such as problem solving and decision making, are based.

McNamara and Kendeou (2011) point out that "behavioral studies of individual differences in comprehension indicate that skilled and less-skilled readers differ primarily in terms of inference processes such as solving anaphoric reference, selecting the meaning of homographs, processing garden-path sentences (i.e., temporarily ambiguous), and making appropriate inferences while reading." In other words, the ability to inference is inextricably linked to comprehension and as such, students who struggle with inferencing skills will have difficulty comprehending what they read. The authors describe major findings from the research literature that include the importance of inference ability in reading comprehension and importantly, describe how teachers can scaffold these skills – even before students are reading to learn.

*The inextricable relationship between background knowledge and inference*

Most authors omit some details in the text they write; therefore, in order to fully comprehend the text, the reader is required to make inferences (i.e., fill gaps). To do this, the reader must draw on background knowledge. Information conveyed through the evidence activates prior background knowledge. Oakhill and Yuill (1996) highlight the role of general knowledge—both experiential and domain-based—to make inferences. Hogan et al. (2011) illustrate the role of experiential knowledge to understand the following sentences.

> Molly carried the glass of juice.
> She tripped on the step.
> Mom fetched the mop.

Why did Molly's mom fetch the mop? The answer to this question is based on inference. Though not stated explicitly in the text, the fact that mom fetched the mop suggests that Molly's misstep with the glass of juice caused it to spill requiring the use of a mop. In other words, the reader's prior experiential knowledge should allow the reader to infer that Molly spilled the juice.

Another example shows how domain knowledge (e.g., background information about weather) is required to fully understand this micro-excerpt from the true story, *The Wild Parrots of Telegraph Hill* (Bittner, 2004).

> Just before Christmas that year, an unusual cold spell hit The Bay Area. It rarely freezes in San Francisco, but **one night the temperature fell to twenty-eight degrees**. As it grew colder, I started worrying about the parrots. I'd been impressed by their tenacity, but it seemed to me that an actual freeze **would surely be their doom.**

To understand this passage—and why the conditions would be the parrots' doom (highlighted yellow)—the reader needs to understand that a temperature below thirty-two degrees is below freezing and could be dangerous to the parrots (i.e., their doom). Without that knowledge about the temperature at which things freeze, the fact that the temperature fell to twenty-eight degrees would not elicit concern by the reader about the parrots' welfare, that is to infer the parrots might freeze to death. In fact, as stated previously in our discussion of background knowledge, a lack of general knowledge is one of the primary reasons for inferencing difficulties (Oakhill and Yuill, 1996).

Elbro and Buch-Iversen (2013) used the following passage to illustrate another aspect of gap-filling, namely, how to understand the connection between pieces of information within the text.

Most people have once heard grasshoppers sing in the summer. The grasshoppers' song is very high pitched. Therefore, **you need a good sense of hearing in order to hear the song**. Actually, it is not correct to say that grasshoppers sing because they do not use their voice to sing. The grasshopper makes the song, or the sound, by rubbing its legs against a sharp edge on the wings. It is not easy to spot a grasshopper as its body is almost invisible when it is surrounded by plants. It blends in with the surroundings. If you want to find a grasshopper, you ought to follow the sound. Remember to listen to the grasshopper while you are young, because **you might not hear the grasshopper when you get older**.

To understand the two pieces of information highlighted in the text—and the humor involved – the reader must fill a gap in the information. This latter information must come from the reader because it isn't in the text.

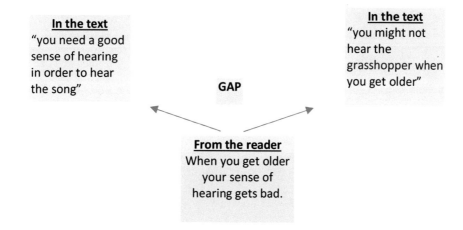

Knowing this information—namely that hearing declines with age—underscores the role and importance of background knowledge. Without that knowledge, fully comprehending and appreciating the passage is impossible.

*When the background knowledge isn't domain knowledge*

The ability to make inferences is also influenced by a reader's 'theory of mind,' which refers to the ability to understand one's own and others' mental states, especially their beliefs and desires. An earlier discussion of text structure (See *The dynamics that drive a narrative* page 17) refers to the use of the critical thinking triangle (CTT) to support the child's comprehension of narrative structure.

One of the three elements of the CTT is the characters' internal responses and feelings to the initiating event. This element of story grammar is integrally related to another element – the characters' mental state(s). In order to comprehend a story, a child must understand what the characters think and want which includes the social/emotional dynamics of the characters' actions and reactions. Inferences that require an understanding of the characters' inner states are influenced by the readers' theory of mind. In the familiar story, *Goldilocks and the Three Bears*, the child must understand why Goldilocks enters the bears' home (e.g., she is hungry, inquisitive, a risk-taker) in order to understand why she essentially breaks into their home without permission. A reader who lacks this understanding sees the characters' actions as a series of events but doesn't connect those actions to the characters' emotions and desires. In this case, the reader will also miss the gist and the moral of the story, namely, that it is important to respect the property of others.

*Visualization*

Readers who create mental images as they listen to or read text are better able to remember and comprehend the text. This is especially true for stories as the reader (or listener) encounters different characters in a variety of settings involved in a series of actions. To support visualizing, students can be taught to explore visual images and texts using a series of questions that support their ability to notice and remember details and use their observations to help them think critically. Both of these skills lead to improved reading comprehension (Dillon, 2009). The following statements can be used to guide the visualization process:

When I look closely at this image,

**I see** _____. (something that jumps out at you in the image)

**I notice** _____. (something you don't think other people will see)

**I think** _____. (an interesting thought you had about this image)

**I wonder** _____. (something you want to know about this image)

We can use these statements to develop an interpretation beyond the actual details in the image. In essence, the viewer is creating a narrative from an image. The following is an example using a painting.

**I see** <u>a ship in turbulent seas.</u>

**I notice** <u>that the waves are washing over the ship.</u>

**I think** <u>experiencing a storm at sea would be terrifying and would require courage to survive.</u>

**I wonder** <u>what happened to the ship and the people on board.</u>

We can also use these statements to activate our knowledge about an image prior to reading. For example, this process could be used prior to reading *The Wild Parrots of Telegraph Hill* to activate background knowledge about parrots.

**I see** <u>a congregation of wild parrots.</u>

**I notice** <u>that the parrots look like they are talking.</u>

**I think** <u>the wild parrots are sociable birds.</u>

**I wonder** <u>why the parrots chose this location in San Francisco to congregate.</u>

Ultimately, the visualization process can (should) be applied to text. Since the goal of this process is to activate imagery about text in the reader's mind, this process is applicable for a variety of texts – from code-emphasis text to full-length novels. Using the first page of *In the Den* (Lauren, 2019), a code-emphasis text, the visualization questions can help readers create images about the text even when the vocabulary and story are limited by the adherence to the decodability of the words.

> On the deck, the kids had a bag.
> A mom had a black hat.
> Yum! Let's pick gum and a pop.

**I see** kids with bags, mom wearing a black hat, and some candy.

**I notice** the characters are outside.

**I think** this might be Halloween because of the bag, the black hat, and candy.

**I wonder** what costumes the kids are wearing.

In this last example, the visualization questions guide readers to notice details and use their background knowledge to create meaning beyond the words, which is the goal of inferential thinking.

*Instructional considerations to foster inferential thinking*

Inferential thinking requires the use of **visual and text clues** combined with background knowledge. One goal of instruction to is to foster students' ability to make inferences by developing their understanding—and expectation—that the text does not contain all of the necessary information to comprehend the text. To simulate this kind of thinking with emerging readers, instruction can use visual cues, rather than text, to encourage gap-filling thinking. Pictures and riddles can provide practice activating what students know to solve visual and verbal puzzles. (See **What Is It?** pages 147 – 152 and **Use What You Know** pages 153 – 158.)

Dewitz, Carr and Patberg (1987) used a **cloze strategy** in their research to help students develop inferential thinking. The strategy, in which a word is strategically omitted, requires students to integrate their background knowledge and text information to generate a plausible response to fill the cloze blank. **The researchers used the following cloze example as part of the research study:**

The car skidded out of control and crashed through the railing over the _____.

Using semantic, syntactic, and world knowledge, possible answers include **highway, river,** or **embankment.** The addition of another sentence following the cloze blank further refines and clarifies the possible responses.

*The car skidded out of control and crashed through the railing over the _____. The boat below was halfway under the bridge and missed being hit.*

What word in the blank makes sense now? Adding the information about the boat, the likely target response would be a **river** or some other body of water.

The results of the researchers' study showed that students who learned to use the cloze strategy made greater gains in comprehension than those who did not use the strategy. In addition to **comprehension** gains, students who learned the cloze strategy also demonstrated greater metacognitive awareness.

Cartwright (2015) recommends the use of a graphic organizer to concretely represent the "missing information" in text. Based on the work of Elbro and Buch-Iversen (2013) mentioned earlier, the graphic organizer (See Figure 7) is designed to "help students visualize the gaps in the information provided in texts and show how the students' own knowledge contributes to their understanding of text." The goal of the approach is to teach "how to use background knowledge in the context of gap-filling inferences" to improve reading comprehension.

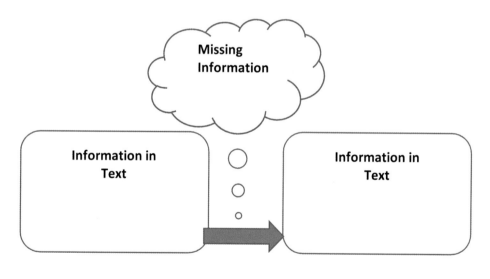

Figure 7

Let's use the graphic organizer to visually represent the missing information in the micro-excerpt about the parrots we looked at earlier. In this example (Figure 8), the missing information is the general information that thirty-two degrees is freezing. This explains the significance of the temperature of twenty-eight degrees, which is below freezing.

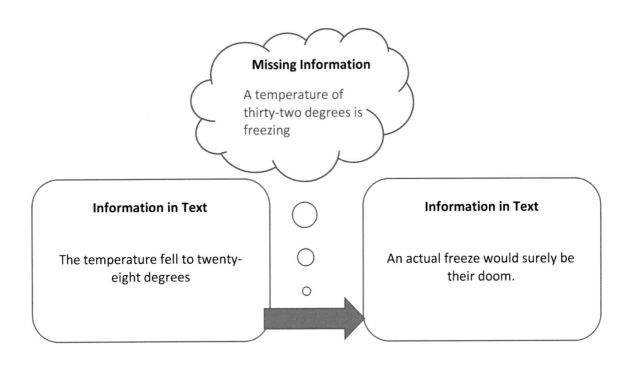

Figure 8

In another approach, Marzano (2010) proposes that teachers use a process to guide students in their thinking when they make inferences. The questions both heighten students' awareness of what goes into making an inference and increase self-monitoring in terms of what is involved in inferential thinking. Marzano's proposed process uses four questions to facilitate the development of awareness and monitoring of inferential thinking: (1) What is my inference? (2) What information did I use to make this inference? (3) How good was my thinking? and (4) Do I need to change my thinking?

Let's apply this process to our excerpt from *The Wild Parrots of Telegraph Hill*.

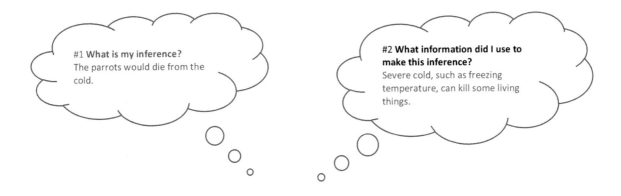

Just before Christmas that year, an unusual cold spell hit The Bay Area.
It rarely freezes in San Francisco, but one night the temperature fell
to twenty-eight degrees. As it grew colder, I started worrying about the parrots.
I'd been impressed by their tenacity, but it seemed to me that an actual freeze
would surely be their doom.

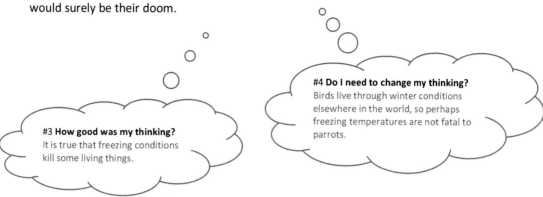

#3 **How good was my thinking?**
It is true that freezing conditions
kill some living things.

#4 **Do I need to change my thinking?**
Birds live through winter conditions
elsewhere in the world, so perhaps
freezing temperatures are not fatal to
parrots.

These questions can be effectively incorporated into read alouds to model the aspects of the process. This explicit instruction in inferencing skills will boost listening and reading comprehension.

## Reading-Writing Connection

*Why writing is important in the development of reading comprehension*

The National Reading Panel's (NRP) meta-analysis of over 200 reading comprehension studies yielded an important finding – the most powerful learning strategy for elementary students was summarizing (Shanahan, 2019). Since the NRP's findings were released in 2000, additional studies have supported the importance of teaching summarizing to young students – first at the oral level and then in writing. The research also demonstrates that this skill is quite difficult because it requires the reader to distinguish between important and unimportant information in order to create a new coherent representation of the text.

Graham and Hebert found in their meta-analyses *Writing to Read* (2010) that "students' reading comprehension is improved by having them increase how often they produce their own text." In other words, writing improves reading comprehension. Hochman and Wexler (2017) explain, "when students write, they—and their teachers—figure out what they don't understand and what further information they need." Writing reveals gaps and misconceptions in the writer's grasp of a topic, requires critical thinking, and generally deepens and strengthens the knowledge a writer begins with (Graham & Perin, 2007).

The Common Core State Standards (CCSS) have brought increased attention over the past decade to the importance of reading and writing informational text beginning in kindergarten. And with this emphasis, there has been an increased opportunity to write about the domain content that students are reading, viewing or listening to. Hochman and Wexler (2018) advocate embedding writing activities in the content being taught as much as possible "to check students' comprehension and deepen their understanding." Jennings and Haynes (2018), who stress theme-centered writing instruction, point out the value of this type of instruction to simultaneously build content knowledge, vocabulary and fluent writing skills. Lemov stresses in his introduction to *The Writing Revolution* (Hochman & Wexler, 2017), "Writing and content knowledge are intimately related. You can't write well about something you don't know well. The more students know about a topic before they begin to write, the better they'll be able to write about it. At the same time, the process of writing will deepen their understanding of a topic and help cement that understanding in their memory."

*The role of the sentence*

"If a reader cannot derive meaning from individual sentences that make up a text, that is going to be a major obstacle in text-level comprehension" (Scott, 2009). Eberhardt (2013) points out that "the sentence is the unit of language strategically positioned between individual words and text. The sentence provides the linguistic environment in which we make decisions about word meaning (e.g. distinguishing between the multiple meaning for words like duck), use of punctuation (e.g., tress versus tree's versus trees'), and the impact of morphological elements (e.g., nominalization of a verb through suffixation, such as revolution from revolt). The sentence is also the language structure in which we can see how the order or arrangement of words has an impact on meaning. For example, the arrangement of words in sentences lets us determine who is doing what to whom (e.g., *The cat chased the dog* versus *The dog chased the cat*). Simply put, context is required to understand the meaning, form, roles and relationships of words. Minimally, context is found within a sentence."

*Sentence expansion – making the abstract concrete*

A simple sentence composed of a subject plus a predicate (S + P) or a subject plus predicate followed by an object (S + P + O) is the most basic structure. To add clarity and precision—that is to supply more information—we can tell more about the action by using adverbs, or more about the subject by using adjectives. Despite the foundational nature of the base sentence, recognizing and writing complete and more elaborated sentences can be elusive for many students. Instructors can make the process of writing a sentence more concrete by using manipulative sentence strips. Paper strips are paired with meta-cognitive guiding questions, which cue the writer to the type of information that builds the sentence (e.g., the question words *who* or *what* identify a person, place, thing or idea; *where* elicits a word or phrases indicating location). This practice can increase how well students develop the critical concept of sentence formation (Greene, 2010).

Consider the following example from *The Wild Parrots of Telegraph Hill* (Bittner, 2004). The process begins by answering the questions that will generate the base sentence.

**Who (what) did it?**

flock

**What did they (he/she/it) do?**

flew in

Additional manipulative pieces and questions serve to expand the base sentence. The following questions help students to elaborate on the predicate. (It is important to note that not every expansion question need be answered for each sentence, hence the blank boxes.)

**Where?**

from the south

**When?**

around dawn

**How?**

usually

After expanding the predicate, questions guide expansion of the subject:

**How many?**

the

**Which one?**

of colorful parrots

**What kind?**

Using the manipulative pieces, students can arrange the words and phrases to compose sentences, and they can vary the syntax (i.e., the word sequence) for clarity and interest. It is possible to arrange the sentence parts in multiple ways. Once arranged, students can compare the meaning of these various configurations: Are they communicating the same meaning or something different?

*The flock of colorful parrots usually flew in from the south around dawn.*

*Around dawn, the flock of colorful parrots usually flew in from the south.*

Through manipulation of sentence parts, students learn to recognize the changes in meaning that can occur when we vary the order of words and phrases. Students become more proficient at producing sentences of increased complexity. As they do so, they enhance their capacity to process complex sentences when listening and reading.

*Unpacking sentence content for understanding and phrasing*

Sentence expansion questions play the reciprocal role of improving reading comprehension. Gottwald (2013) expressed it well by equating micro-level sentence analysis to basic comprehension. For example, the same questions about the function of words in sentences can be used to unpack (i.e., break down text to understand it) a sentence to identify its subject (*What is doing it?*) and verb (*What does it do?*). Consider our sentence:

*Around dawn, the flock of colorful parrots usually flew in from the south.*

| What is doing it? | flock |
| --- | --- |
| What did it do? | flew in |
| How did it fly? | usually |
| Where did it fly in? | from the south |
| When did it fly in? | around dawn |
| How many? | the |
| Which flock? | of colorful parrots |

Analysis designed to extract meaning provides the added benefits of increasing students' interaction with the text (i.e., repeated readings) and helping them parse the language into meaningful units (phrases). They can thereby increase their use of phrasing when reading. In the following sentence, slashes denote phrases.

*Around dawn/, the flock/ of colorful parrots/ usually flew in/ from the south.*

Practicing this skill during reading instruction helps students develop the automaticity that enables them to apply phrasing when reading complex text. (See *Syntax: Knowledge to Practice* for more activities to develop sentence expansion abilities.)

*The importance of summarizing*

Writing (or telling) summaries is one of the instructional practices shown to be effective in improving students' reading comprehension. "For students in grades 3 – 12, writing summaries about text showed a consistently positive impact on reading comprehension" (Graham & Hebert, 2010). Summarizing, the act of producing a brief statement of main points about text or graphics, offers a number of benefits because of the abilities required to do it. Hochman and Wexler (2017) delineate the following ways summary writing is powerful:

- Boosts reading comprehension

- Helps generate concise and accurate responses to questions

- Maintains focus on the main idea and supporting details

- Teaches paraphrasing techniques

- Provides practice synthesizing information from multiple sources

- Enhances the ability to analyze information

- Develops the ability to make generalizations

- Aids in retaining information.

Cartwright (2015) explains that "skilled comprehenders are able to produce good summaries of texts that they read, which preserve the most important aspects of meaning of longer texts. ...to extract the 'gist' or meaning from connected language (e.g., summarization), executive functions are needed to prioritize the importance of information and inhibit irrelevant details, and working memory [is needed] to hold information in storage during transformation."

Hochman and Wexler (2017) emphasize the common ground between summarizing and sentence expansion. Both practices require determining "what's most important in a given body of information, what details support the main idea, and how the details relate to one another." The act of determining what to include in a summary seems to improve comprehension of the content being summarized.

The authors used the sentence expansion questions (See *Sentence expansion – making the abstract concrete* pages 46 – 47) in the following template to support the development of a sentence summary (See Figure 9).

Figure 9

**Sentence Summary**

Name:_____ Date:_____

who/what: ................................................................................................................................

(did/will do) what: ....................................................................................................................

when: ........................................................................................................................................

where: .......................................................................................................................................

why: ..........................................................................................................................................

how: ..........................................................................................................................................


**Summary Sentence:**

_____

_____

_____

_____

Used with permission from Hochman & Wexler (2017)


Using information and vocabulary from our text excerpt from *The Wild Parrots of Telegraph Hill,* the template serves as a graphic organizer by providing a scaffold to gather key information to include in the summary sentence. (See **Sentence Summaries**, pages 161 – 172.)  It can also be used to help students plan before writing, even for a single-sentence summary (Wexler, 2019) by bridging the retrieval process of topic content and the process of using that information to compose sentences (See Figure 10).

Figure 10

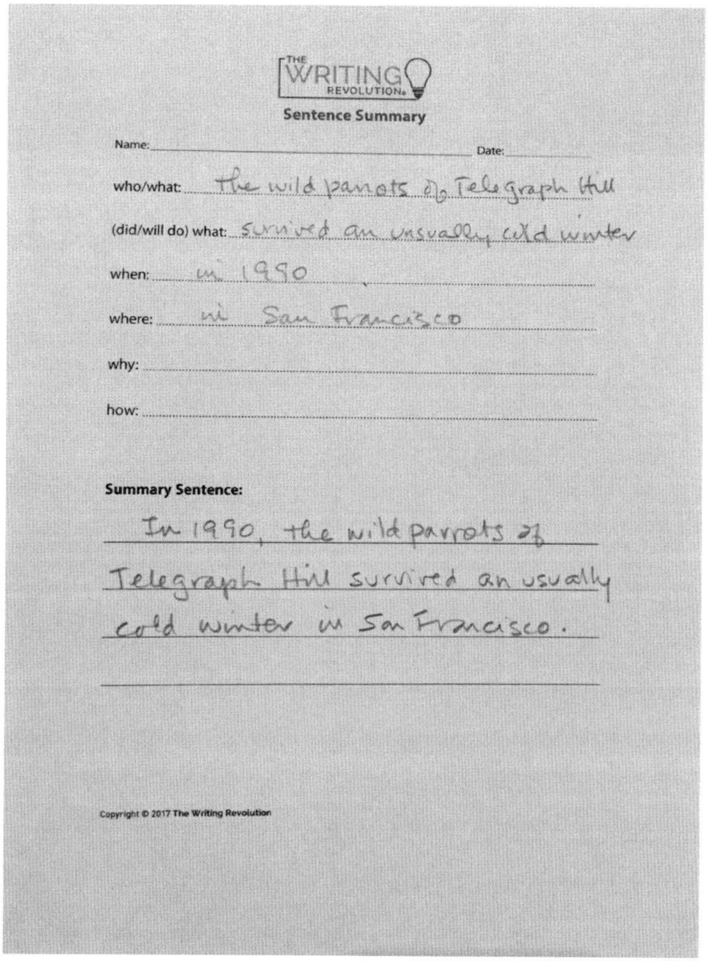
THE WRITING REVOLUTION

**Sentence Summary**

Name: ______________________ Date: __________

who/what: the wild parrots of Telegraph Hill

(did/will do) what: survived an unsually cold winter

when: in 1990

where: in San Francisco

why: ______________________

how: ______________________

**Summary Sentence:**

In 1990, the wild parrots of Telegraph Hill survived an usually cold winter in San Francisco.

Copyright © 2017 The Writing Revolution

Lane (2019) suggests that effective note-taking is an excellent way to promote good summarizing, because the act of writing notes requires putting content into the readers' own words. Combined with the use of text structures (e.g., a Story Map) to organize the notes, students produce summaries that reflect their understanding of the story or information. (See the activities **Story Map** pages 110 – 124 and **Knowledge Trees** pages 125 – 138.)

*The academic language of questions*

The key to question interpretation is knowledge of the academic language used to form queries. For example, the following table illustrates the required content in the answer for the frequently used "W" questions words.

| Question word | Content required in answer | Examples |
|---|---|---|
| Who/what | A name of person, place, thing or idea | girl, Mr. Jones, the queen, my friend |
| Did what | The action that happened | ate, wondered, grew |
| When | A time | on Halloween, once upon a time, the next morning |
| Where | A location | on the deck, in the den, to the market, New York |
| How | The way something was done | happily, very sadly, suddenly |
| Why | A reason | because she was hungry, because he was too young |
| Which | Descriptive information about the namer | a festival of sun celebration, whole grain foods |

Students will be more likely to provide accurate and complete answers when they understand how to respond to questions beginning with these academic question words. In addition, these w/wh questions require students to reason, hypothesize, and predict.

Students require direct, explicit instruction to learn the relationship among the text they have read, the "W" questions they have asked, and the responses that use the text and the academic language of the question. This process applies to content from both narrative and informational text. Answering "W" questions based on narrative text reinforces the elements of a story. For example, **who** questions tap recall of characters in the story; **did what** questions draw on actions in the plot; **when** and **where** questions require understanding of the features of setting. In contrast, when readers apply the "W" questions to nonfiction text, they elicit factual information and contribute to their acquisition of knowledge. (See **What's the Answer?** pages 173 – 184). This reading – writing relationship based on text-based content is crucial to developing background knowledge essential to comprehension (Hochman & Wexler, 2017).

Initially, an emphasis on the "W" questions guides readers to get the "gist" of the text (Beck, 2015), or surface-level understanding. The CCSS, however, have made it necessary for teachers to ask higher-order questions that require analyzing and critical thinking. These questions model the thinking processes that students must engage in independently in order to comprehend complex text. Hess and her colleagues (2009) introduced educators to the term *cognitive rigor* which 'encompasses the complexity of content, the cognitive engagement with that content, and the scope of the planned learning activities." The model that these authors reference is Webb's Depth-of - Knowledge (DOK) which expands on Bloom's taxonomy. The DOK model focuses on knowledge of content as well as the skills that are required to complete a specific task, while Bloom's describes the type of thinking that is needed to answer a question. Both models provide a hierarchy of academic language used for prompts and questions. Given the fact that our students are expected to comprehend complex text, including content-rich informational text, questions that require strategic thinking and reasoning and involve more than one possible answer will encourage critical thinking required to boost 21$^{st}$ century skills.

*Instructional emphases to use writing to develop comprehension*

In their large-scale review of research on the relationship between reading and writing mentioned earlier, Graham & Hebert (2010) recommended the following:

- Have students write about the texts they read, including writing notes, summaries and answers about text they listen to or read.
- Increase how much students write to build fluency in writing skills and processes, along with building knowledge from text.

Writing activities to develop comprehension for beginning readers should focus on explicitly utilizing the text to write. At this early stage, teachers should place less emphasis on students' volume of writing and more on guiding them to use text to produce a written product.

## A Postscript About Writing

Although the full scope of skills and processes required to be a proficient writer are not covered within this book, it is essential to teach students all the writing skills and processes that go into creating text, including handwriting and spelling (i.e., transcription skills), as well as sentence and paragraph construction (i.e., text generation). (See *Phonemic Awareness and Phonics: Knowledge to Practice* for more about spelling instruction and *Syntax: Knowledge to Practice* for more about sentence development.)

Berninger and Winn's 'Not-So-Simple View of Writing' model (2006) pictured here (Figure 11) shows a triangle that represents three aspects of written expression (lower-level transcription skills, higher-level text generation skills, and executive functions required to manage the process in order to produce a well-organized and well-written text). The original triangle depicted what was considered a simple view of writing; however, working memory was added to the center of the triangle to represent the complexity of the writing process. Many researchers, including Berninger and Winn, confirm that writing is the most difficult of all literacy and language skills. To quote Johnson and Myklebust (1967), "writing is acquired the latest, mastered by the fewest, and learned with the most effort over the longest period of time."

Figure 11

## The Not-So Simple View of Writing Model
## (Berninger & Winn, 1996)

Text Generation

Working
Memory[a,b]

COGNITIVE FLOW

**Transcription**
(handwriting,
keyboarding,
and spelling)

**Executive Functions**
(supervisory attention,[c]
goal setting, planning,
reviewing, revising,
strategies for self-
monitoring and regulating)

Sedita (2019) uses an adaptation of Scarborough's reading rope (Hollis Scarborough's "Reading Rope")
to convey the multiple components necessary for skilled writing, which helps to illustrates why writing is so
challenging. (See Figure 12.) As with the components of reading included in the reading rope, each of the writing
components delineated here require explicit and ongoing instruction for students to acquire proficiency.
Fortunately, many of the components required for skilled writing play a reciprocal role in the development of
reading comprehension.

Figure 12

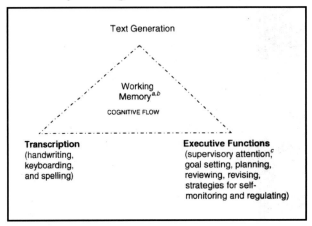

**The Strands That Are Woven Into Skilled Writing**
*(Sedita, 2019)*

**Critical Thinking**
- Generating ideas, gathering information
- Writing process: organizing, drafting, writing, revising

**Syntax**
- Grammar and syntactic awareness
- Sentence elaboration
- Punctuation

**Text Structure**
- Narrative, informational, opinion structures
- Paragraph structure
- Patterns of organization (description, sequence, cause/effect, compare/contrast, problem/solution)
- Linking and transition words/phrases

**Writing Craft**
- Word choice
- Awareness of task, audience purpose
- Literary devices

**Transcription**
- Spelling
- Handwriting, keyboarding

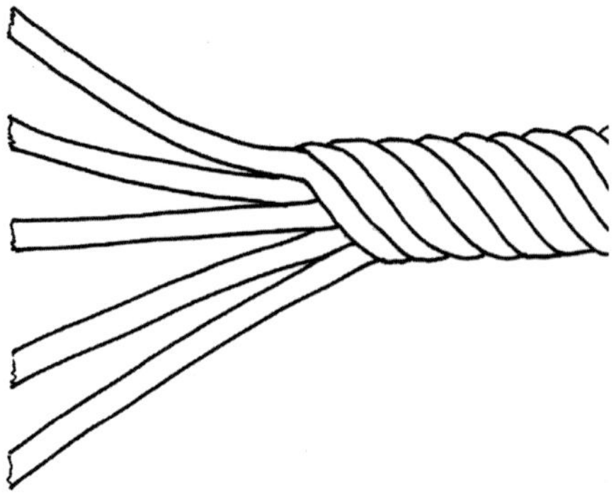

Used with permission from Sedita (2019).

 **Text Selection and Analysis**

## The Changing Roles of Text Across the Stages of Reading Development

The demands, uses and types of text change as children progress from Stage 0 to 2. (See the table on the following pages). Stage 0 features predictable text that is based on oral language patterns and structures. Predictable literature provides instructional opportunities for children to develop their vocabulary, grammatical awareness, and background knowledge, all of which contribute to comprehension. In contrast, code-emphasis (.e. decodable) text is designed specifically to promote children's mastery of the speech-to-print dimensions of reading in Stage 1. Decodable text is potentially less engaging in terms of its narrative or informational interest, but it is critical to developing fluent reading. Engaging with code-emphasis text is to the beginning reader much like practicing scales is to the novice piano player: simple content allows the beginner to learn the basic skills that underlie the capacity to read/play more complex and richer material. Stage 2 features the use of authentic text, which represents the vast majority of print material. The instructional focus is on content, including story structure and the concepts and details found in informational structures. Since students at Stage 2 can decode, teachers can shift instructional focus at the word level to strategies for determining word meaning. (For more information about these three types of text, see *Phonics: Knowledge to Practice* in the Literacy How Professional Development Series.)

*Comprehension at every stage*

Comprehension is a component of instruction and learning during every stage of reading development. While it is true that the Stages of Reading Development detailed by Chall emphasize word attack as the focus during Stage 1, this is not to suggest that decoding is the only important aspect of reading development during this stage. Some aspects of comprehension can—and should—be developed orally through read aloud and other listening or visually-oriented activities before students can decode (i.e., Stage 0) and during the time that students focus on mastering the code (i.e., Stages 1 and 2). And even though the focus in Stage 1 is on learning to decode—both single words and code-emphasis (decodable) text—comprehension should still be part of the instructional plan. Decoding words accurately and automatically without attention to meaning is never recommended. Doing so contradicts the ultimate goal of reading which is to make meaning.

We know that the text we choose plays an important role in phonics instruction, namely to provide opportunities for students to master the application of the phoneme-grapheme knowledge they are acquiring by reinforcing the "lesson to text match." (See *Phonemic Awareness and Phonics*: *Knowledge to Practice*.) So too, the types of text have implications for comprehension instruction. Regardless of the Stage, each type of text—predictable, code-emphasis or authentic—lends itself to comprehension development. Additionally, listening comprehension instruction can – and should – occur during all stages using text that is read to students. This greatly expands instructional possibilities to develop the big ideas involved with comprehension development.

The following table provides an overview of each type of text in terms of its characteristics, purpose, and impact on becoming a proficient reader.

| | Stage 0<br>Predictable | Stage 1<br>Code-emphasis | Stage 2<br>Authentic |
|---|---|---|---|
| Characteristics | • Syntactic repetition<br>• Use of concrete pictures that reflect meaning<br>• Relies on use of syntactic and semantic cues (i.e., patterns familiar from spoken language) | • High proportion of words with phonically regular relationships between letters and sounds<br>• High degree of match between the letter/sound relationships represented in text and those that the reader has been taught (i.e., phonics instruction)<br>• Value of code-emphasis text is contingent upon the degree to which the phonics lessons and the code-emphasis text are aligned | • Word selection based on the content of the story or information rather than specific syntactic or phonetic features |

| | Stage 0<br>Predictable | Stage 1<br>Code-emphasis | Stage 2<br>Authentic |
|---|---|---|---|
| **Purpose** | • Bridges the transition from spoken to written language to help children understand the relationship between spoken and written language<br>• Supports learning concepts of print (i.e., directionality, word boundaries, finger-point reading) | • Helps readers transition from a pre- and partial alphabetic stage to a more balanced word identification approach, including alphabetic knowledge<br>• Supports the readers' efforts at word identification<br>• Provides for application of letter/sound knowledge that students have learned to connected text.<br>• Directs the reader's attention to letters and sounds | • Provides text to apply word identification skills to increase accuracy and automaticity<br>• Uses more varied and complex sentence structure to facilitate the development of prosody (i.e., reading with phrasing based on meaning-based units) |

| | Stage 0<br>Predictable | Stage 1<br>Code-emphasis | Stage 2<br>Authentic |
|---|---|---|---|
| **Sample text** | The following excerpt from a poem illustrates features of predictable text. This text uses repetition of words and phrases. The structure of each stanza repeats with the substitution of a different food, making it easier for children to "read" the text.<br><br>*The Hungry Girl*[1]<br><br>"No! I'm hungry!"<br>Said the little girl<br>To her dearest dad<br>"Would you like to taste this toast?<br>That's what your brother had."<br><br>"No! I'm hungry!"<br>Said the little girl<br>To her dearest dad<br>"Would you like to munch a muffin?<br>That's what your bother had." | The following sentences illustrate highly controlled code-emphasis text.<br><br>The den is not lit.<br>It is dim and black. [2]<br><br>This text uses a combination of<br><ul><li>High frequency words (**the** and **is**) usually memorized in early grades because they use less-common letter-sound associations (e.g., **s** representing / **z** /)</li><li>Words composed of letters representing their most frequently used sounds (e.g., consonants t, d, m, n, bl-, -nd (blends) and –ck for / **k** /; short vowel sounds for a, i, o and e); letter-sound associations that students would have learned by the time they attempted to read the sentence.</li></ul>The decodability of these sample sentences is predicated on the phonetic regularity of the words and the match to previous phonics instruction, referred to as the Lesson-to-Text Match.[3] | The following excerpt illustrates authentic text.<br><br>*Jack and the Beanstalk*[4]<br><br>"Once upon a time there lived a poor widow who had an only son named Jack. She was very poor, for times had been hard, and Jack was too young to work. Almost all the furniture of the little cottage had been sold to buy bread, until at last, there was nothing left worth selling."<br><br>This text uses a combination of<br><ul><li>High frequency words (e.g., **once, there, who, was**)</li><li>Low frequency, content-specific words (e.g., **widow, cottage**)</li><li>Words composed of a more advanced level of phonic elements (e.g., lower-frequency vowel patterns such as **or** as in **work** and **worth**)</li><li>Words with morphological elements (e.g., **-ed** in **lived** and **named**)</li><li>More syntactically complex sentences requiring parsing (i.e., phrasing) of words into meaningful phrases and clauses</li><li>Pronoun referents (e.g., **she** for **widow**) to promote text cohesion</li></ul> |

[1, 4]www.ReadWorks.org
[2]*In the Den* by Jill Lauren (2020)
[3]The Reading League Webinar *Deciphering Decodable Text* (2019)

*Concurrent paths – learning to decode and developing comprehension through listening*

While students are learning to decode fluently enough so they can ultimately 'read to learn', that is, to learn content from reading, they can access content through various types of listening activities. Interactive read-alouds—an approach in which students listen to adults read and participate in a discussion about the text—are an "incredibly effective method for supporting children's literacy learning (Wright, 2019)." Teachers reading to students takes on an important role in comprehension instruction, particularly before students are proficient decoders. Listening to text provides a means for students to build knowledge and vocabulary and learn about text genre as they master the code.

Creating code-emphasis text on informational topics for Stage 1 readers is particularly difficult. In addition to the limited decoding skills of beginning readers, subject-related vocabulary rarely adheres to a carefully sequenced progression. Potentially, this contributes to Stage 1 students experiencing delays in acquiring background knowledge. To circumvent this problem, Wright proposes reading to students sets of texts that are conceptually or thematically related. She reports that researchers have shown that this approach can be "particularly beneficial for building knowledge (2019)." (See *How to develop background knowledge with beginning readers* on pages 28 – 29.)

Fisher and Frey (2014) point out that decades of research "confirm that listening comprehension outpaces reading comprehension from early childhood through at least middle school." (See Figure 13.) This fact further supports using listening-level texts as part of a comprehensive plan not only with beginning readers but also through the intermediate and middle school years.

Figure 13

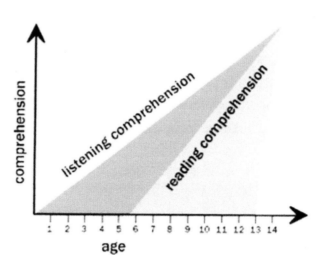

Listening and Reading Comprehension by Age
(Stricht & James,1984)

Castles et al (2018), who discuss the relationship between listening and reading comprehension, underscore the importance of supplementing what students can read themselves in order to build their background knowledge. The authors note that as word recognition improves, reading comprehension becomes hampered by limitations in background knowledge and the ability to create a mental model, regardless of whether the language is heard or read (LARC, 2015). "This demands a range of spoken-language skills, often subsumed under the general construct of 'listening comprehension'; in skilled readers, the correlation between listening comprehension and reading is almost perfect (e.g., Gernsbacher, Varner, & Faust, 1990)."

*The value of read-alouds*

Drawing on the work of Sticht, Hirsch (2003) explains that "oral comprehension typically places an upper limit on reading comprehension." The implication, he adds, is that "oral comprehension generally needs to be developed in our youngest students if we want them to be good readers." To do this, he contends that "before students can read substantive texts on their own, this content will be best conveyed orally." The solution, in part, is the use of read-alouds that can immerse beginning readers in word and world knowledge, laying the foundation for future reading comprehension.

When considering read-alouds as part of reading instruction, Wright (2019) outlines several key features to consider. The first is that read-alouds should be interactive, meaning "that the teacher and students are actively involved in thinking and talking about the read-aloud text." Next, effective read-alouds are those that are "purposeful and planned." For this to happen, teachers must engage in cognitive preparation, including careful selection of the text and how it will be used, which is discussed in more detail in the following sections. Finally, Wright suggests that "effective interactive read-alouds can and should occur across the school day, in a broad range of content areas, and not just during language arts." Wright also contends that students continue to benefit from read-alouds even after they can read independently. "This is because the texts that beginning readers use for practice purposefully limit challenging vocabulary to make the text easier to decode. Therefore, while students are learning to decode fluently, teachers can promote vocabulary and world knowledge development by reading aloud from texts that are more challenging than the texts that students can read by themselves."

# Preparing Text to Develop Comprehension

*Selecting text to use for instruction*

Teachers face several important decisions when choosing text for instructional purposes. In *"The changing roles of text across the Stages of Reading Development"* section (See pages 55 – 59), we established that **every** type of text selection—predictable, code-emphasis, and authentic—presents opportunities to work on comprehension. To illustrate this, we used each type of text for the activities in "Activities for Instruction and Informal Assessment" (See pages 110 – 184).

Mesmer (2017) poses another dimension when considering text selection. She explains "there are two different types of texts that are used in lessons—those that teachers write themselves (construct) and those that come from authentic sources (e.g., textbooks, trade books, web-based passages). Both are essential for instruction, but for different purposes."

1. For initial instruction in a skill, strategy or concept, teachers often use or write constructed practice texts for an explicitly targeted instructional objective. We are familiar with this approach with the use of code-emphasis text (i.e., decodable) when students are given practice using specific sound-spelling correspondences (i.e., Lesson to Text Match).

2. Authentic text offers excellent opportunities to practice comprehension skills in context. For instance, an informational selection may include examples of pronoun connectives, making it possible for students to identify the chain of references to identify cohesion in the text. In other cases, a narrative selection may require students to draw upon background knowledge to be able to make inferences about what is happening in the story and why/how the characters respond to specific events.

Regardless of the type of text, cognitive preparation, *the intentional act of using knowledge of comprehension demands of text to maximize instructional time through the use of the selected text*, is required. Next, let's look at aspects of that preparation.

First a few general guidelines for teachers before we practice looking at text with an eye to its potential to develop language processing to develop comprehension:

1. Before using any text, read it.

2. Decide which comprehension "big idea" to focus on based on the text selection or on explicit instruction students have had.

3. Identify a portion of the text to use to illustrate and teach text processing as an essential comprehension skill. Use of micro-discourse, namely segments of text a few sentences in length, keeps instruction focused on a manageable amount of text.

4. Be selective. Less is more. Limit the scope of instructional objectives for any given selection. Wright encourages teachers to do this to help keep students engaged in the lesson and to increase the likelihood that they can achieve the lesson's goal.

5. Be sure students have had explicit instruction in a strategy before applying it to a text selection.

Next, select vocabulary as part of the cognitive preparation process. Include child-friendly definitions/explanations in the planning documents. Wright explains that students "learn and retain more words when teachers provide child-friendly explanations of new vocabulary." But, she points out that this practice is more effective when teachers plan these explanations—along with pictures, props or actions—before the read-alouds, because it can be challenging to spontaneously think of child-friendly explanations.

Then, use the text analysis cue questions suggested below that help zero in on the five big ideas of comprehension. Each of the big ideas has us looking and thinking differently about the text.

*Using big idea cue questions with narrative text*

Below we've illustrated how cue questions can help us analyze text by using micro-discourse excerpts from *The Empty Pot* (Demi, 1990), a narrative text example.

**Text Structure Awareness**

Cue question to ask about the text: *How is the text organized?*

A long time ago in China there was a boy named Ping who loved flowers.
Anything he planted burst into bloom. Up came flowers, bushes, and even
big fruit trees, as if by magic!

Everyone in the kingdom loved flowers too.

They planted them everywhere, and the air smelled like perfume.

The Emperor loved birds and animals, but flowers most of all, and he tended his own garden every day.

The elements of a story—setting, characters and a problem—are clues that this text is organized as a narrative.

An instructional goal is to help students identify these elements of the story.

Instructional consideration:

Use a graphic organizer to record the words and phrases that signal the elements of story grammar. See the **Story Map** activity pages 110 – 124 for more about how to teach narrative structure.

The Problem

**But the** Emperor was very old. He needed to choose a successor to the throne.

Who would his successor be? And how would the Emperor choose? Because the Emperor loved flowers so much, he decided to let the flowers choose.

The next day a proclamation was issued: All the children in the land were to come to the palace. There they would be given special flower seeds by the Emperor. "Whoever can show me their best in a year's time," he said, "will succeed me to the throne.

...................................................................................................

## Background knowledge needs

Cue question to ask about the text: *What word/phrase/sentence is essential to understand the story?*

 What were we thinking?

But the Emperor was very old. He needed to choose a successor to the throne.

Who would his successor be? And how would the Emperor choose? Because the Emperor loved flowers so much, he decided to let the flowers choose.

The next day a proclamation was issued: All the children in the land were to come to the palace. There they would be given special flower seeds by the Emperor. "Whoever can show me their best in a year's time," he said, "will succeed me to the throne."

The word **successor** is critical to understanding the story. Using a potentially more familiar word **succeed** to help learn **successor** models using morphological connections.

Instructional consideration:

Select words based on morphological elements to link a familiar word (e.g., succeed) with a less-familiar word (e.g., successor). Instruction can also point out that **succeed** is a multiple meaning word. Students may be familiar with a more familiar meaning (i.e., to achieve what you want) rather than the meaning in this context (i.e., to take over a person in a job or position). See the **Word Selection Grid** in *Vocabulary: Knowledge to Practice* for more about selecting words for vocabulary development.

.......................................................................................................................................

## Cohesive ties

Cue question to ask about the text: *Who/what is the person, thing or idea that this micro-passage is about?*

**Referential**: trace noun/synonym (highlighted) and pronoun connections (in **bold**)

But the Emperor was very old. **He** needed to choose a successor to the throne. Who would **his** successor be? And how would the Emperor choose? Because the Emperor loved flowers so much, **he** decided to let the flowers choose.

 What were we thinking?

Identifying and tracing the main character using synonyms and pronouns contributes to understanding who the story is about.

Instructional consideration:

Review how writers use pronouns to refer to or replace nouns. See the **Text Links** activity pages 139 – 145 for more about teaching cohesive ties in text.

Cue question to ask about the text: *Are there causal, intentional, or temporal connections in this micro-passage?*

**Deep**: causal, intentional, and temporal connectives help the reader to form a more coherent and deeper understanding of the text. Also gives clues to the text structure (e.g., narrative)

A long time ago in China there was a boy named Ping who loved flowers. Anything he planted burst into bloom. Up came flower, bushes, and even big fruit trees, as if by magic!
Everyone in the kingdom loved flowers too. They planted them everywhere, and the air smelled like perfume. The Emperor loved birds and animals, but flowers most of all, and he tended his own garden every day.

But the Emperor was very old. He needed to choose a successor to the throne. Who would his successor be?

 What were we thinking?

Some words and phrases—**a long time ago** and **the next day**—indicate a temporal sequence of events. These particular phrases are often used as part of telling a story, so they give a clue that this excerpt is from a narrative.

The other highlighted words—**but** and **because**—signal causation. In this excerpt, they signal the problem of the story.

And how would the Emperor choose? Because the Emperor loved flowers so much, he decided to let the flowers choose.

The next day a proclamation was issued: All the children in the land were to come to the palace. There they would be given special flower seeds by the Emperor. "Whoever can show me their best in a year's time," he said, "will succeed me to the throne."

Instructional consideration:

Review how writers use words and phrases to connect information and ideas in text. Point out how a phrase like "a long time ago" is used in telling a story. Brainstorm other phrases often used in telling stories (e.g., once upon a time).

..................................................................................................

## Inferential thinking

Cue question to ask about the text: *What gap does the reader need to fill to understand the text?*

"Where you got your seeds from, I do not know. For the seeds I gave you had all been cooked. So it was impossible for any of them to grow.

 What were we thinking?

Gap filled: The flowers the other children had could not have been from the seed the Emperor gave the children, because cooked seeds will not grow.

Key to understanding the story is the inference that Ping was the only one who had used the seed the Emperor had given him because he didn't have a flower. The flowers grown by the other children had to be different seeds, ones that weren't cooked. The Emperor found Ping to be an honest person because he didn't have a flower to show. Instructional consideration:

Emphasize the background information that can inform an inference in the text. In this case, a brief explanation about how seeds grow can help students appreciate how the Emperor chose Ping as his successor.

..................................................................................................

**Reading/Writing Connection**

Cue question to ask about the text: What namer (noun) and action (verb) can we use to write a sentence summary?

When Ping received his seed from the Emperor, he was the happiest child of all. He was sure he could grow the most beautiful flower. Ping filled a flowerpot with rich soil. He planted the seed in it very carefully. He watered it every day. He couldn't wait to see it sprout, grow, and blossom into a beautiful flower. Day after day passed, but nothing grew in his pot. Ping was very worried He put new soil into a bigger pot. The he transferred the seed into the rich black soil. Another two months he waited. Still nothing happened. By and by the whole year passed.

 What were we thinking?

Selecting the name of a main character (**Ping**) and a key action carried out by the character (**planted**) provides a base sentence starting point to summarize the story.

Instructional consideration:

Guide students to use the sentence expansion questions (**Tell Me More – Action** and **Tell Me More – Namers**) based on information from the text to write a detailed sentence summary. See **Sentence Summaries** pages 161 – 172 for more about teaching sentence-length summaries.

Now, let's repeat this process with an informational text selection. We can ask the same questions about informational text to help identify possible challenges in the text or to reinforce instruction that helps students develop text understanding.

As we look at this example, we should keep in mind an important distinction between narrative and informational text, namely that an informational text can present the reader with multiple text structures within the same selection. In our example using *A Plant Puzzle*, we illustrate this as we consider how the text is organized.

**Text Structure Awareness**

Question to ask about the text: *How is the text organized?*

 What were we thinking?

In order for a plant to grow, it needs three very important puzzle pieces: water, carbon dioxide, and light. Plants use their roots to take in water from the ground. They use their leaves to take in sunlight and carbon dioxide from the air.

These two paragraphs from *A Plant Puzzle* present the reader with two different text structures—descriptive and sequence.

The function of a descriptive structure is to explain something. In this case, the descriptive paragraph tells us what plants need to grow.

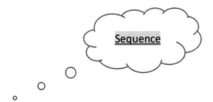

The function of a sequential text structure is to explain how something happens. A clue to this organization is the word "process," which signals a sequence of steps.

Plants use these three puzzle pieces to make their own food in a process called photosynthesis. Using the energy from the sun, these living organisms convert water and carbon dioxide into sugar. This sugar feeds the plant's growth from a seedling into an adult. In the process, the vegetation releases oxygen into the air.

Instructional consideration:

Use of a graphic organizer—even at the paragraph level—can help illustrate the differing ways that the information in the text is organized. A web-type organizer for the descriptive paragraph is different than a list-type organizer that would be used for the process paragraph and can occur within the same informational text selection. See "Features of Informational Text Structures" pages 22 – 24 for an array of organizational patterns and corresponding visual organizers.

## Background knowledge needs

Cue question to ask about the text: *What word/phrase/sentence is essential to understand the story?*

What were we thinking?

Plants use these three puzzle pieces to make their own food in a <u>process</u> called ░photosynthesis░. <u>Using the energy from the sun</u>, these living organisms <u>convert water and carbon dioxide into sugar</u>. This sugar feeds the plant's growth from a seedling into an adult. In the process, the vegetation releases oxygen into the air.

Content-specific vocabulary is an important vehicle for building background knowledge. In this excerpt, the word **photosynthesis** is the essential term to learn.

Instructional consideration:

Often content-specific vocabulary is defined within the text. Learning to use signal words and morphological cues in text can help students determine the meaning of the new terms. For more about using the context to define new words, see *Vocabulary: Knowledge to Practice* for Word Learning Strategies.

.................................................................................................................................

## Cohesive ties

Cue question to ask about the text: *What is the person, thing or idea that this micro-passage is about?*

**Referential**: trace synonym and pronoun connections (in bold)

What were we thinking?

**Plants** use these three puzzle pieces to make **their** own food in a process called photosynthesis. Using the energy from the sun, **these living organisms** convert water and carbon dioxide into sugar. This sugar feeds the **plant's** growth from a seedling into an adult. In the process, the **vegetation** releases oxygen into the air.

A repeated word or phrase signals what the whole passage is about. Often writers use synonymous words or phrases (i.e., **plants, these living organisms, and vegetation**) and pronouns (i.e., **their**). It is important to recognize these synonyms and pronouns to identify what a passage is about.

Instructional consideration:

During informational text read alouds, explicitly point out synonyms. For example, in this selection the teacher could say, "**These living organisms** means the same thing as **plants**. We can substitute **plants** for **these living organisms** and the text will mean the same thing."

Cue question to ask about the text: *Are there causal, intentional, or temporal connections in this micro-passage?*

**Deep**: causal, intentional, and temporal connectives help the reader to form a more coherent and deeper understanding of the text. Also, gives clues to the text structure (e.g., narrative)

Since only certain plants grow in hot, cool, wet, or dry climates, each environment is made up of different types of plant life. A desert may grow palm trees and cacti, while a forest may grow tall pines or oak trees.

 What were we thinking?

These two sentences from *A Plant Puzzle* provide two examples of words (i.e., subordinating conjunctions) that signal a cohesive tie. The word **since** signals the relationship between climates and the type of plant life that will thrive there.

The second sentence illustrates the use of **while** to indicate a switch from what grows in the desert to what grows in the forest.

Instructional consideration:

Words signaling deep cohesive ties are also effectively addressed during informational read alouds. For example, the teacher could explain the meaning of the word **since** by rephrasing the sentence using a more familiar subordinating conjunction, such as **because**. The teacher might say, "**Since**, or **because**, only certain plants grow in hot, cool, wet or dry climates, each environment is made up of different types of plant life."

## Inferential thinking

Cue question to ask about the text: *What gap does the reader need to fill to understand the text?*

 What were we thinking?

Plants use their <u>roots</u> to take in water <u>from the ground</u>.

Gap filled: Roots are the part of the plant under the ground.

Plants use these three puzzle pieces to make their own food in a process called <u>photosynthesis</u>. <u>Using the energy from the sun</u>, these living organisms <u>convert water and carbon dioxide into sugar</u>.

Gap filled: Photosynthesis means light (sun) processing (convert water and carbon dioxide into sugar) for a plant to make food to grow.

To understand how plants get water from the ground, the reader needs to know the parts of the plant and that roots are under the ground. Understanding text requires using background knowledge, which often is based on knowing the vocabulary associated with the content.

Instructional consideration:
Using morphological information that cuts across content domains (e.g., **photo** in photosynthesis, photography, telephotography) can be helpful in acquiring new terminology.

......................................................................................................................................

## Reading/Writing Connection

Cue question to ask about the text: What namer (noun) and action (verb) can we use to write a sentence summary?

 What were we thinking?

In order for a plant to grow, it needs three very important puzzle pieces: water, carbon dioxide, and light. Plants use their roots to take in water from the ground. They use their leaves to take in sunlight and carbon dioxide from the air.

Plants use these three puzzle pieces to make their own food in a process called photosynthesis. Using the energy from the sun, these living organisms convert water and carbon dioxide into sugar. This sugar feeds the plant's growth from a seedling into an adult. In the process, the vegetation releases oxygen into the air.

Selecting **plant** (namer) and **use** (action) requires students to write a summary sentence that focuses on the main idea of the text.

Instructional consideration:

Guide students to use specific content from the text to expand the base sentence. Encourage students to go back to the text for content details.

*Using big idea cue questions with code-emphasis text*

Students can begin to develop meaning-making habits whenever—and with whatever—they are reading, including code-emphasis (decodable) text. For example, when students are reading decodable words to practice accuracy and automaticity, they should also be thinking about what the words and the text mean. Let's apply the cue questions to an excerpt from *Buzz, Buzz* (Lauren, 2018), a code-emphasis text.

**Text Structure Awareness**

Cue question to ask about the text: *How is the text organized?*

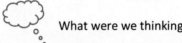

What were we thinking?

The elements of a story—setting, characters—are clues that this text is organized as a narrative.

An instructional goal is to help students identify the elements of the story.

Instructional consideration:

Use a graphic organizer to record the words and phrases that signal the elements of story grammar. See the **Story Map** activity pages 110 – 124 for more about how to teach narrative structure.

Gus is on the bus.

A bug is on the bus.
Buzz, buzz, buzz.

Gus is off the bus.

**Background knowledge needs**

Cue question to ask about the text: *What word/phrase/sentence is essential to understand the story?*

Gus will have a fun run.
But the bug **bugs** Gus.
So, he runs to his tub.

 What were we thinking?

Understanding what **bugs** means is key to the main character's behavior.

Instructional consideration:

Instruction can also point out that **bug** is a multiple meaning word. Students may be familiar with a more familiar meaning (i.e., an insect) more than the meaning in this context (i.e., to annoy someone).

........................................................................................................................

**Cohesive ties**

Cue question to ask about the text: *What is the person, thing or idea that this micro-passage is about?*

**Referential**: trace synonym and pronoun connections (in bold)

 What were we thinking?

**Gus** will have a fun run.
But the bug bugs **Gus**.
So, **he** runs to **his** tub.

In a story, authors often use pronouns (i.e., **he**, **his**) in place of a character's name (i.e., Gus). It is important to recognize these synonyms and pronouns who the story is about.

Instructional consideration:

During narrative text read alouds, explicitly point out the use of pronouns. For example, in this selection the teacher could say, "**Gus** is the main character in our story. The author used **he** and **his** to refer to **Gus**. We can substitute **Gus** in the sentence – So, Gus runs to Gus's tub. and the text will mean the same thing."

Cue question to ask about the text: *Are there causal, intentional, or temporal connections in this micro-passage?*

**Deep**: causal, intentional, and temporal connectives help the reader to form a more coherent and deeper understanding of the text. They also give clues to the text's structure (e.g., narrative).

Gus will have a fun run.
But the bug bugs Gus.
So, he runs to his tub.

 What were we thinking?

This excerpt from *Buzz, Buzz* provides two examples of words that signal a cohesive tie (i.e., coordinating conjunctions). The words **but** and **so** signal a causal relationship. **But** in the second sentence signals something opposite from the first sentence—having fun from being bugged.

The third sentence illustrates the use of **so** to indicate another causal relationship—because the bug was bugging Gus, he ran away.

Instructional consideration:

Words signaling deep cohesive ties are also effectively addressed during informational read alouds. For example, the teacher could explain the contrast signaled by the conjunction **but** by saying, "Gus was having fun but that changed when the bug bothered him." Similarly, for the conjunction **so**, the teacher might say, "**So** signals that Gus is going to do something because the bug was bothering him. What did he do? He ran to his tub to get away."

**Inferential thinking**

Cue question to ask about the text: *What gap does the reader need to fill to understand the text?*

Gus will have a fun run.
But the bug bugs Gus.
So, he runs to his tub.

Gap filled: Experiential knowledge suggests that Gus does not like bugs (i.e., they bother him) and wants to get away from this bug.

**What were we thinking?**

Often readers draw upon personal experiences to fill gaps in the text. In this excerpt, the reader will need to understand that Gus was having fun until the buzzing bugs annoyed him. He then ran to his tub to escape the bugs. Most children will be able to identify with Gus' feelings.

Instructional consideration:

Teachers can have students visualize and/or act out having a bug buzzing around and how they would react. Visualization and acting out help students relate to the actions and feelings of characters in the story.

.......................................................................................................................................................................

**Reading/Writing Connection**

Cue question to ask about the text: What namer (noun) and action (verb) can we use to write a sentence summary?

 What were we thinking?

Gus will have a fun run.
But the bug bugs Gus.
So, he runs to his tub

Selecting the name of a main character (**Gus**) and a key action carried out by the character (**runs**) provides a base sentence starting point to summarize the story.

Instructional consideration:

Guide students to use the sentence expansion questions (See *Syntax: Knowledge to Practice* **Action: Tell Me More** and **Namer: Tell Me More**) based on information from the text to write a detailed sentence summary. See **Sentence Summaries** pages 161 – 172 for more about teaching sentence-length summaries.

*Try it!*

Look at the following micro-passages and identify an instructional "big idea" that you might focus on based on the content of the passage. Remember, most excerpts will lend themselves to working on all or several big ideas.

| Big ideas | Cue questions to ask about the text |
| --- | --- |
| Text Structure | How is the text organized? |
| Background knowledge | What word/phrase is essential to understand the story? |
| Cohesive ties | Referential – Who/what is the person, thing or idea that this micro-passage is about? |
| | Deep – Are there causal, intentional or temporal connections in this micro-passage? |
| Inferential thinking | What gap does the reader need to fill to understand the text? |
| Reading/Writing connection | What namer (noun) and action (verb) can be used to write a sentence summary? |

#1      *How Do Seeds Grow?*

Many plants start out as small seeds. How does a seed grow?

First, it falls or is put into dirt. The sun's light helps the seed to grow. The seed gets energy from water.

Before long, the seed breaks open. Roots start to grow down into the dirt. Then a shoot pushes up through the dirt. The stem and leaves pop out next.

Soon, the little plant will be grown-up.

.......

#2      *Starting Over*

Two girls in Sri Lanka walk past the rubble that was once their school. It was destroyed in the tsunami (soo-NAH-mee), or series of huge waves, that hit South Asia in December of 2005.

.......

#3      *The Hungry Girl*

"No! I'm hungry!"
Said the little girl
To her dearest dad
"Would you like some yummy yogurt?
That's not what your brother had."

"Yes I would"
Said the little girl
To her dearest dad
She ate the yogurt by herself,
Which made her brother mad!

.......

#4      A Butterfly's Life

A butterfly's life begins in a special way. First, a mother butterfly lays an egg on a leaf. A caterpillar

hatches from the egg. The caterpillar eats leaves and grows bigger.

......

#5      *The Story of a Snowflake*

First, drops of water in clouds get cold. Next, those drops turn into bits of ice. Then, the bits of ice stick together. They stick together in all kinds of shapes. The shapes get heavy. They fall from the clouds to the ground. We call these icy shapes snowflakes!

We have provided our thoughts for each micro-passage in the Appendix on pages 198 – 200.

## Text Selection Skills Analysis

In addition to the analysis of narrative and informational text selections using the big idea cue questions to identify processing demands, teachers can also use text selections to provide direct instruction designed to improve students' processing abilities.

In this section of *Comprehension: Knowledge to Practice*, we model the use of instructional activities tailored for each comprehension big idea with several text selections. For each selection, we provide a Text Analysis table with examples of domain-specific learning objectives that are applicable for the selection. The table provides learning objectives for multiple domains to illustrate the range of options for using each text. Following the objectives, we draw from activities in the **Index of Activities** to show how to apply the activities to the selection. The **Activity Application to Text** table includes a "Think Aloud" component. The purpose is to provide an example of the thinking teachers might do to select an activity that is designed to target a specific aspect of text processing so that students are better able to construct the meaning of the text. The Text Analysis examples are presented in the order of the activities on page 108.

## The Wishing Tree[1]

Deep in the woods is a secret tree. Only one boy knows about it. It's a wishing tree.

One day, the boy followed his dog into the woods. They stopped at the tree.

"I wish I could climb this tree!" the boy said.

POOF! His wish was granted. He was in the tree!

The leaves began to giggle.

"Hello!" they said. "Pleased to meet you!"

"My name is Noah," the boy said. "What's yours?"

All the leaves started to talk at once.

"We are the Wishing Tree," the leaves said. "We see good children and give them gifts."

"I wish I had one million dollars!" said Noah. But nothing happened.

"I said I wish I had a million dollars!" Noah said, louder.

"We heard you the first time," said the leaves.

"What good are you, anyway?"

"Very good," said the leaves. "This is a very good tree."

"Then give me money!" Noah demanded.

"We can only give you good things. Things that will make you a better person."

Well, that didn't sound like much fun. He thought of a new wish.

"I wish I could fight a dragon!" he said.

"Do you honestly think we would conjure a dragon?" asked the leaves.

"I guess not," said Noah. "Well, then, I wish I were brave enough to fight a dragon!"

Suddenly, Noah was standing at the bottom of the tree.

"Wish granted!" said the leaves.

"Arooo!" said Peanuts the dog.

"Let's go!" said Noah. He and Peanuts ran out of the woods. But Noah didn't feel very brave.

"Some wishing tree that was! No money! No dragons! What a waste!"

Crack! Suddenly, something hit him in the back of his head.

"Hey, No-Brains!" someone was shouting.

"Oh no!" Noah said to Peanuts. "It's Mitch the bully!"

Mitch was throwing peanuts at Noah.

"Here are some peanuts for your dumb dog!" Mitch said.

That was the last straw! Noah couldn't take it anymore.

"Go away, bully!" he yelled. "You never hurt dogs!"

"Aroo!" howled Peanuts the dog.

"Whatever!" said Mitch. "You're not worth my time."

Mitch left.

"Yay! He left!" Noah said. "Thank you, wishing tree!"

Noah had never told Mitch to go away before. But on that day, he was very brave. Being brave was just like fighting a dragon. Being brave was better than having a million dollars.

You see, Noah thought his bravery came from the wishing tree. But the truth is, the tree didn't grant any wishes. Noah did it all himself. Being brave came from inside.

If you could make a wish like Noah, what would you wish for?

Text Analysis

| Vocabulary | Syntax | Comprehension |
|---|---|---|
| • Develop word networks and morphological elements **(granted, brave, bully)** | • Focus on elaborating the namers (nouns) in a sentence | • Identify story grammar elements to develop narrative knowledge <br> • Retell the narrative using story grammar elements on the map |

Activity Application to Text

| Activity Selection "Think Aloud" | Lesson Focus: Comprehension – Identify story grammar elements |
|---|---|
| | Activity: Story Map (See page 112) |
| | Group size: Small or Whole Group |

| *The Wishing Tree* is a narrative text comprised of story grammar elements. The **Story Map** activity provides a guide for teachers and students to identify and record these elements to facilitate recall and retelling the story. Students can use the completed graphic organizer to support their retelling of the story. | **Materials needed**: *The Wishing Tree* text; Story Map template with projector or whiteboard/chart paper for hand-drawn template; sticky notes (3x5" size)<br><br>**How to do activity**:<br><br>1. Display the Story Map graphic organizer. Review with students that the Story Map helps organize what they listen to or read in a story. Describe the parts of the organizer. Review what each part of the organizer represents:<br>  a. The **setting** is where and when the story takes place.<br>  b. **Characters** are the people, animals or creatures who act out the story.<br>  c. **Initiating event**, sometimes referred to as the problem, tells what happens to cause a response that sets a series of other actions in motion.<br>  d. **Reactions/Feeling**: the character's feelings about what happened<br>  e. **The Plan**: what the character plans to do to achieve his/her goals<br>  f. **Actions/Attempts** are the sequence of attempts the character does to carry out the plan.<br>    a. **Consequence** tells what happens as a result of the plan and attempts.<br>    b. **Resolution**: how the character feels about the consequence<br><br><br><br>2. Have students listen to or read *The Wishing Tree*. Using the order of information on the graphic organizer, ask students to tell information from the story. Write what they recall on individual sticky notes. Place the notes on the Story Map.<br><br>3. After the information is placed on the Story Map, read each sticky note with students. |

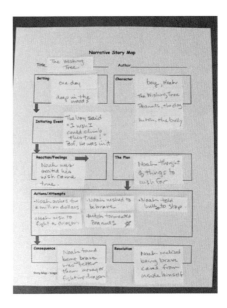

4. Finally, use the graphic organizer to retell the story. Model how to start with the sticky notes for the setting and progress through the remaining elements on the organizer. For example:

> "One day, Noah and his dog Peanuts went for a walk deep in the woods. They came to a tree that Noah said he wished he could climb. All of a sudden he was in the tree. Noah was excited his wish came true and began to think of other things the Wishing Tree could grant him. He wished for a million dollars. No luck. He wished he could fight a dragon. Still no luck. He wished he could be brave enough to fight a dragon. Then a bully named Mitch began to torment Peanuts. Noah told Mitch to stop and he did. Noah found being brave was better than money or fighting a dragon because he liked feeling brave and being able to help his dog."

5. Have several students take turns retelling the story using the information on the Story Map as a guide. Or, have student partners take turns retelling the story to each other.

[1]Go to www.ReadWorks.org for a printable version of *The Wishing Tree*.

Clouds and Rain[2]

Look up at the sky. You may see clouds. What are clouds made of?

Clouds are made of tiny drops of water. Some clouds look white and fluffy. Some clouds look stringy like wisps of hair. Other clouds look gray.

Gray clouds can bring rain. They are made of bigger drops of water. If the drops get too big, they fall from the sky. Now it is raining.

The Story of a Snowflake[2]

Do you know how we get snowflakes? Let's find out. First, drops of water in clouds get cold. Next, those drops turn into bits of ice. Then, the bits of ice stick together. They stick together in all kinds of shapes. The shapes get heavy. They fall from the clouds to the ground. We call these icy shapes snowflakes!

Text Analysis

| Vocabulary | Syntax | Comprehension |
|---|---|---|
| • Sorting words with suffixes (–y and –s) | • To sort words into categories based on function (i.e., namers and actions) | • Select information from text to build background knowledge |

Activity Application to Text

| Activity Selection "Think Aloud" | Lesson Focus: Comprehension – Select information from text |
|---|---|
| | Activity: Knowledge Trees (See page 125) |
| | Group size: Small Group |
| Both informational text selections—*Clouds and Rain* and *The Story of a Snowflake*—provide information about precipitation. The activity **Knowledge Trees** guides students in selecting and categorizing information from informational text. This selection and the classification process used in this activity helps students build background knowledge. | **Materials needed**: **Knowledge Tree** template with project or whiteboard/chart paper for hand-drawn template; text selection *Clouds and Rain* and *The Story of a Snowflake*; sticky notes (3 x 5 size); prepared sticky notes for the topic "precipitation" <br><br> **How to do activity**: <br> 1. Display the Knowledge Tree graphic organizer. Remind students that the Knowledge Tree helps organize information from what they listen to or read. <br><br> <br><br> 2. Review the parts of the organizer: <br>    a. The trunk is where we write the **topic**. The topic is what the whole article is about. <br>    b. The branches are where we write **subtopics**. The branches are categories of information about the topic. <br>    c. The leaves are where we write **details**. The details provide information about the subtopics. Details are often descriptive. <br> 3. Place the prepared sticky note for the topic on the trunk (i.e., kinds of precipitation). <br><br> |

4.  Read *Clouds and Rain* to students and ask them to listen for information they hear in the article. Write what they recall on individual sticky notes. Display the sticky notes as you write them.

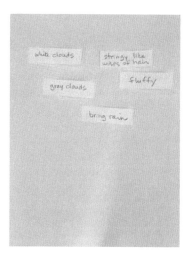

5.  After students recall as many pieces of information as they can, read each sticky note to students and guide them to identify the subtopics. For example, you could ask students what kinds of clouds were mentioned in the selection (i.e., white clouds, gray clouds). Place these sticky notes on the branches of the **Knowledge Tree**. Draw more branches as needed.

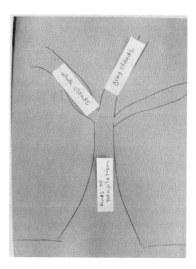

6.  Next guide students in deciding which category a piece of information fits into. Place each note on the Knowledge Tree according to its category (e.g., white clouds – fluffy, stringy like wisps of hair; gray clouds – bring rain)

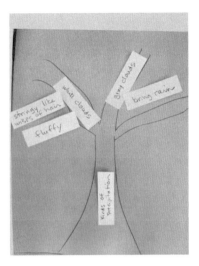

7. After all of the pieces of information are placed on the tree, use the graphic organizer to summarize the content. Model how to start with the sticky note on the trunk and then add a branch and details to create an oral summary. For example:

    "This article is about different kinds of clouds and the type of precipitation that comes from them. Some clouds are white. They are often fluffy or wispy. Other clouds are gray. These often cause rain.

    Have several students take turns stating the summary in their own words.

8. Read other articles to students on the same topic (e.g., *The Story of a Snowflake*). Write information on sticky notes —subtopics and details—that students recall from the new article. Add the additional notes to the Knowledge Tree to build content knowledge about the topic (See notes on orange sticky notes.)

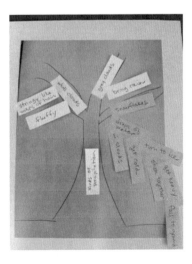

[2]Go to www.ReadWorks.org for printable versions of *Clouds and Rain* and *The Story of a Snowflake*.

86

## Stage 0 – Listening level text

A Trip to the Zoo

My grandmother took me to the zoo on a Saturday in May.
I had so much fun walking around, watching the animals at play!

The colors and sounds, they did abound, as we ambled around the zoo.
I saw so many wonderful sights, some familiar and some brand new.

One colorful peacock spread his feathers beneath a lotus tree.
Two chatty monkeys hung from a branch while they fixed their eyes on me.

Three striped zebras nibbled hay that was scattered upon the ground.
Four lazy lions roamed with their pride but didn't make a sound.

Five elephants played next to a river spraying water oh so far!
And six young cubs slept beside their mother, a bear the color of tar.

Seven giraffes stood in a herd, necks stretching towards the sky.
Eight beady eyes peered from their perch, four owls that didn't fly.

A troop of nine gorillas played and played behind the bars so tall.
And last but not least, ten sea lions swam in a pool and played ball.

As we left the zoo I thanked gramma for spending the day with me.
And I let her know about my plan. A zookeeper I shall be!

Text Analysis

| Vocabulary | Syntax | Comprehension |
|---|---|---|
| • Sort words by category (e.g., mammals, birds) to develop word networks | • Use prepositions to express the relationship (i.e., meaning link) between words | • Use pronouns to connect content across text |

Activity Application to Text

| Activity Selection "Think Aloud" | Lesson Focus: Comprehension – use pronoun referents to build cohesion. |
|---|---|
| | Activity: Text Links (See page 139) |
| | Group size: Small Group |
| The poem *A Trip to the Zoo* includes an abundance of pronouns to make connections within and across sentences. The **Text Links** activity provides an opportunity to illustrate the use of pronouns as cohesive ties with each verse of the poem. | **Materials needed**: *A Trip to the Zoo* on chart paper or projected with a document camera<br><br>**How to do activity**:<br>1. Review with students that there are words that we use instead of our real people names or the names of objects. These words are called pronouns. We use them instead of namers. For example, instead of saying "**Grandma** and **I** went to the zoo", we could say "**We** went to the zoo." The word **we** is a pronoun that refers to **Grandma** and **me**. (Provide other examples as needed.) Writers use pronouns to make their writing more interesting.<br><br>2. Display the poem. Have them follow along as you read each verse of the poem to them.<br><br>3. After reading the verse, highlight the pronouns in the text (they and we). Help students to identify what each pronoun refers to (i.e., **they** refers to **colors** and **sounds**; **we** refers to **grandma** and **me**). To make this reference concrete, draw an arrow from the pronoun to the word or words they refer to.<br><br>The colors and sounds, they did abound, as we ambled around the zoo.<br>I saw so many wonderful sights, some familiar and some brand new.<br><br>4. Repeat the process with each verse of the poem. |

Our New Old House[3]

Boom!

A clap of thunder made the old house shake. Ramon huddled under the covers of his bed. A jagged streak of lightning lit up the room. I hate this house, Ramon thought. It was his first night in his new home. The house had belonged to his grandma. It was very, very old. Paint peeled off of the walls. The wood boards of the floor creaked when you walked on them.

The house looked really creepy at night, Ramon thought. The trees outside his windows looked like monsters in the dark. Their branches looked like long arms. They waved when the wind blew. The storm made everything extra creepy. Ramon hated storms anyway. But it somehow seemed worse in the old house.

Ramon pulled the covers off of his head. The thunder became quieter. Ramon drifted off to sleep. When he woke up, sun was streaming through his window. Ramon yawned and climbed out of bed.

The trees outside didn't look like monsters anymore. The branches had nice green leaves growing on them. Ramon could see a bird sitting on one of the branches. It chirped a happy song.

Ramon walked to the window and looked outside. It looked pretty nice in the daylight. A bubbling stream cut across the yard. A tire swing hung from one of the trees. A garden of flowers grew next to the tree. Butterflies flew around the flowers. "Maybe living here won't be so bad after all," Ramon said.

Text Analysis

| Vocabulary | Syntax | Comprehension |
|---|---|---|
| • Develop word networks and morphological elements (granted, brave, bully) | • Use coordinating conjunctions (i.e., **and**, **or**, **but**) to join words, phrases, and clauses | • Use background knowledge to make inferences |

Activity Application to Text

| Activity Selection "Think Aloud" | Lesson Focus: Syntax – To develop awareness of the role that coordinating conjunctions play in connecting words, phrases, and clauses in a sentence |
| --- | --- |
| | Activity: Use What You Know (See page 153) |
| | Group size: Small Group |
| *Our New Old House* is a narrative text that requires students to have background knowledge about what a storm might sound and feel like in an old house. *Use What You Know* is an activity that engages students in sharing what they know and are thinking while they read the text. | **Materials needed**: the story *Our New Old House* projected; chart paper or white board<br><br>**How to do activity**:<br><br>1. Tell students that when they read, they need to use what they know to understand what the story they are reading is about.<br>2. Select a portion of the text and display it for the students to see. |

Ramon pulled the covers off of his head. The thunder became quieter. Ramon drifted off to sleep. When he woke up, sun was streaming through his window. Ramon yawned and climbed out of bed.

Ask students to identify what they know from the text. Make notes of their observations on the T-chart under "What is in the text?"

| What is in the text? | What do I think is happening? |
| --- | --- |
| Ramon had the covers over his head<br><br>there was thunder<br><br>sun was streaming through his window | |

3. Tell students that even though the text doesn't say it, we can figure out what is happening in the story. Ask students to suggest what the clues from the text might mean is happening. Record their ideas on the T-chart.

| What is in the text? | What do I think is happening? |
| --- | --- |
| Ramon had the covers over his head | Ramon was frightened |
| there was thunder | there was a strong storm that frightened Ramon |
| sun was streaming through his window | the storm ended; Ramon was happier |

4. Ask students to explain what is happening (e.g., Ramon covered his head because he was frightened by the storm).

5. Explain that their ideas about what is happening in the text—even though it isn't written—are called inferences. For example, we infer that Ramon is frightened because he covers his head during the thunderstorm. We use what we know to try to figure out what isn't in the text.

6. Repeat with another portion of the story.

[3]Go to www.ReadWorks.org for a printable version of *Our New Old House*.

## A Butterfly's Life[4]

Butterflies are beautiful insects. You often see them around colorful flowers.

A butterfly's life begins in a special way. First, a mother butterfly lays an egg on a leaf. A caterpillar hatches from the egg. The caterpillar eats leaves and grows bigger.

Next, the caterpillar spins a covering around itself. The covering is called a chrysalis. Inside the chrysalis, the caterpillar slowly changes. The parts of a butterfly begin to form, like the wings, legs, and antennae.

About two weeks later, a new creature pops out of the chrysalis. It has become a butterfly! The butterfly flutters its wings and flies away.

Text Analysis

| Vocabulary | Syntax | Comprehension |
|---|---|---|
| • Word Learning Strategies: Meaning Clues (Signal word cues)<br>• Review Picture Clues and Word Clues | • Generating and expanding complete sentences (subject + predicate + object) using namers (i.e., nouns) and actions (i.e., verbs)<br>• Determine impact of word order on the meaning of content. | • Use content from text to write summary sentences |

Activity Application to Text

| Activity Selection "Think Aloud" | Lesson Focus: Comprehension – use content from informational text to compose expanded sentences |
|---|---|
| | Activity: Sentence Summaries using Informational Text (See page 159, 171) |
| | Group size: Small Group |
| *A Butterfly's Life* is an informational text using namers and actions to provide subject-matter content about butterflies. These namers and actions can be the basis for summarization. In the **Sentence Summaries** activity, students expand the namer and action using a questioning process and drawing information from the passage. | **Materials needed**: *A Butterfly's Life* text in a displayable format; notecards or sentence strips<br><br>**How to do activity**:<br>1. Display the text selection for all students to see. Read the selection to the students.<br>2. Remind students that they can use what they know about namers (nouns) and actions (verbs) to build sentences. Review that combining a namer and an action creates a complete thought.<br>3. Provide students with a namer and action and object based on the content of the story.<br><br>butterfly    lays    egg<br><br>4. Review that we can tell more about the action (i.e., **lays**) to make the sentence more interesting and accurate. To tell more about the action, we answer the following questions:<br><br>• When? *When* tells a specific time or period of time when the action happens.<br><br>• Where? *Where* tells a specific or general location where the action happens.<br><br>• How?   *How* tells the way in which something is done.<br><br>5. Have students tell more about the action (i.e., **lays**) based on content from the story (e.g., **on a leaf** tells *where* the butterfly lays the egg). Write the word or phrase on a card or sentence strip to add to the sentence.<br><br>on a leaf<br><br>6. Review that we can tell more about the namer (i.e., plants) to make the sentence more descriptive. To tell more about the namer, we answer the following questions:<br>• How many? Tells a specific number or refers to an indefinite number.<br>• What kind?  Describes observable (e.g., color, shape, size) or not observable (e.g., smart, kind, grouchy) attributes.<br>• Which one?  Distinguishes from among named people, places or things (e.g., this, that, my). |

7. Have students tell more about the namer (i.e., energy) based on content from the story (e.g., **mother** tells *what kind* of **butterfly**). Write the word or phrase on a card or sentence strips to add to the sentence.

|  |
| --- |
| mother |

8. Arrange the cards to expand the simple sentence. Capitalize the first letter. Add a period at the end. Have students read the expanded sentence.

| | | |
| --- | --- | --- |
| The mother | caterpillar | lays |

| | |
| --- | --- |
| an egg | on a leaf. |

9. Repeat the process with other simple sentences based on the selection.

⁴Go to www.ReadWorks.org for a printable version of *A Butterfly's Life*.

**ACTIVITIES for Instruction and Informal Assessment**

Features of effective instructional practices

Effective, evidence-based practices, which are associated with a structured literacy approach, are applicable to comprehension instruction. These practices allow us to address both aspects of comprehension instruction—**what to teach** and **how to teach it**. Let's look at how these features apply to comprehension instruction.

- **Explicit instruction**: Explicit instruction means direct teaching of content, strategies, and skills. In the case of comprehension, explicit instruction focuses on both content (e.g., key vocabulary, language use) and procedures (e.g., identifying information based on text structures). Comprehension instruction should include teaching students to recognize signal words associated with different text structures. For example, with narrative text, the focus is usually on the language that the author uses to tell the story. In contrast, with informational text, the focus is on the content knowledge. Some words and phrases signal a story, such as **once upon a** time. In contrast, **first**, **next**, and **last** often signal a sequence of facts in informational text. Other words/phrases are particularly helpful to readers because they signal the kind of information required to answer a question (e.g., A question beginning with the word "who" requires the name of a person in the response. See the activity **What's the Answer** pages 173 – 184.) Explicit instruction also focuses on teaching students to select and record information from text selections based on macro level text structures associated with narrative and expository texts. These processes help students understand and remember what they read. (See the activities **Story Map** pages 110 – 124 and **Knowledge Trees** pages 125 – 138.)

- **Emphasis on making abstract concepts concrete:** Using multisensory and multimodal techniques (i.e., visuals and graphics) helps make abstract concepts and content concrete. For example, graphic organizers representing genre structures (i.e., narrative versus informational) provide guidance to readers about the organization of the selection's content. (See the activities **Story Map** pages 110 – 124 and **Knowledge Trees** pages 125 – 138.) Pictures are an effective tool to teach inferencing. For example, students can gain an understanding of the difference between literal information (e.g., what is in the picture, such as a popped balloon) in contrast to what isn't in the picture but can be inferred (e.g., something made the balloon pop). (See activities **What Is It?** page 147 – 152 and **Use What You Know** page 153 – 158.)

- **Emphasis on automaticity**: Every aspect of literacy improves with attention to automaticity. In the case of comprehension, the combination of accurate and automatic word recognition, as well as grouping words into phrases, contributes to increased fluency, prosody and understanding. When students make progress from word-by-word reading to reading words in meaningful groups, the rate of reading improves, and equally important, comprehension increases as evidenced through the phrasing. (See *Syntax: Knowledge to Practice* for more about phrase building. See **Action: Tell Me More** and **Namer: Tell Me More** activities.)

- **Development of meta-cognitive strategies**: As with other aspects of literacy development, using meta-cognitive strategies—the awareness or analysis of what one is reading—plays an important role in developing comprehension. An example of a meta-cognitive strategy is the interpretation and use of connectives when reading. The realization that pronouns refer to an antecedent (another noun) in the text is essential for successful comprehension. Attention to cross-text connectives (i.e., text cohesion) is one way students can monitor their understanding of what they are reading. (See activity **Text Links** pages 139 – 145.)

- **Stress on cumulative, systematic, and sequential presentation of content and skills**: Unlike other domains of literacy development, such as phonics or grammar in which there are a finite set of content elements to learn, comprehension is a domain that is unconstrained – that is, with infinite scope. Despite this difference, building knowledge through wide reading on a topic that follows a content scope and sequence is critically important to comprehension. Through systematic and repetitive exposure to content area vocabulary and concepts, students are better prepared for the inferential demands of text, namely the ability to read between the lines of literal meaning. (See the activity **Knowledge Tree** pages 125 – 138.) Another example of cumulative, systematic and sequential presentation of content and skills focuses on a plan of instruction using strategies appropriate for *before, during* and *after* reading a text selection.

- **Use of data to guide instruction**: Comprehension is the ultimate goal of reading instruction. In contrast to gathering data about a discrete body of knowledge such as in phonics (e.g., 44 speech sounds, 26 letters of the alphabet) or grammar (e.g., eight parts of speech), measuring comprehension is more complicated. Teachers often use standardized measures, but informal procedures aligned to aspects of explicit instruction are likely to yield better information for instructional planning. For example, a retelling rubric can provide feedback regarding a student's selection and recall of story content. Or, a summary-telling rubric can provide feedback regarding a student's selection and recall of content from informational text. (See The Role of Retelling Rubrics in Monitoring Student Progress in Comprehending Text pages 99 – 102.)

## Constrained vs. Unconstrained – Implications for Instruction

Learning letter-sound relations and identifying both lower- and uppercase letters are examples of constrained skills, because the number of elements to be mastered is small and finite. Vocabulary and comprehension, on the other hand, are considered unconstrained skills because the number of elements are infinite, and as such, will never be mastered entirely. For example, using coordinating conjunctions (and, but, for, nor, or, so, and yet) is one way to increase text complexity by combining simple sentences into a compound sentence. Once students have a basic understanding of these conjunctions, their use conveys another layer of meaning as in the following sentences in which **but** signals a change in direction in meaning.

> The temperature dropped below freezing. The parrots didn't perish.
> The temperature dropped below freezing, **but** the parrots didn't perish.

Despite the expectation that freezing temperatures might be perilous to the parrots, it wasn't. The use of **but** conveyed that contrast.

Hochman and Wexler (2017) advocate practice with coordinating conjunctions embedded with content. By doing so, students acquire background knowledge and simultaneously develop the syntactic skills necessary to read and write complex text.

They illustrate this with the following example from American History:

> Abraham Lincoln was a great president **because** _____.
> Abraham Lincoln was a great president **but** _____.
> Abraham Lincoln was a great president **so** _____.

> Possible responses based on a grasp of historical knowledge:

> Abraham Lincoln was a great president **because** *he kept the North united during the Civil War.*
> Abraham Lincoln was a great president **but** *many Americans didn't like him while he was alive.*
> Abraham Lincoln was a great president **so** *more books have been written about him than any other American leader.*

This difference in the type of skills involved with comprehension instruction impacts lesson planning and the role of assessment. Lesson planning for comprehension development must stress cumulative and sequential content and skills applied to increasingly more complex text. Informal assessment must focus on evidence of students' acquisition of comprehension's "big ideas" namely use of text structure to recall and retell text, awareness of cohesive devices to grasp the gist of texts' meaning, and use of background knowledge to make inferences. This type of skill acquisition is not linear but iterative, taking into account the integration and application of many aspects of literacy development concurrently.

## An Important Distinction: Comprehending Text Versus Answering Comprehension Questions

Asking questions of students before, during and after reading (or listening) is often used as part of comprehension instruction, but the ability to answer questions correctly is dependent upon understanding the text in the first place. Different skills are required for each—comprehending text and answering comprehension questions—and both have instructional implications. Let's take a look at this distinction at the three points in the reading process—before, during, and after.

| | Before | During | After |
|---|---|---|---|
| **Comprehending Text**: depends on interacting with text before, during and after reading text to extract (acquire) both surface level and deep understanding. At the core of comprehending text is processing the language at the semantic (vocabulary), syntactical, and content knowledge levels. | | | |
| Genre and text structure awareness | Distinguish between genre—story versus informational text | Use graphic organizers representing different genre (See **Story Map**; **Knowledge Trees**) and text structures (e.g., time sequence; cause/effect; comparison) | Give oral summary utilizing genre structure features (See **Story Map**; **Knowledge Trees**) |
| Knowledge – Comes from:<br>• Experiences (e.g., activities, visiting places)<br>• Listening to stories<br>• Watching videos | Identify topic of text. Inquire what students know about the topic. | Read to students and gather information about the topic (See **Knowledge Trees**) | Review knowledge from text and add information from other sources to deepen knowledge base.<br><br>Say or write summaries (See **Sentence Summaries**) |
| Text cohesion | | Use referential and deep cohesive ties to understand the text (See **Text Links**) | |
| Inference | | Relate background knowledge to fill gaps in meaning (See **What Is It?** and **Use What You Know**) | |
| **Answering Comprehension Questions**: depends on understanding and remembering text | | | |
| Interpreting questions | Use prediction questions (e.g., based on title – *What do you think this story/article is about?*; *What might we learn about ____?*) | Use prediction questions (stories) – *What will happen next?* [Note: less easy to predict while reading with informational text] | Focus on surface level knowledge questions to check understanding of the gist of the text. (See **What's the Answer?**)<br><br>Locate information in text—stories or informational (See **What's the Answer?**) |

# The Role of Retelling Rubrics in Monitoring Student Progress in Comprehending Text

Teachers often assess students' comprehension by asking them to orally retell the content, including the gist, of a reading selection. The teacher evaluates the retelling by recording details that the students include and by judging the coherence of the retell. A set of criteria that guides rating these details and specific points that are given in the retelling are the basis of the rubric. As such, retelling rubrics—as a form of progress monitoring—are more aligned with the "big ideas" of comprehension than answering questions after reading text. For this reason, we recommend retelling rubrics rather than multiple choice, open ended questions, or cloze formats for assessing comprehension, especially for emerging readers whose reading proficiency often is insufficient to manage the requirements of these other assessment formats.

Rubrics help structure the way we examine students' efforts at recalling and retelling what they listen to or read. This type of assessment tool can also capture students' language usage, as well as their grasp of the key features of various text structures—narrative or informational. In addition, rubrics can be used to gauge how well the student organizes and internalizes the content of the text selection and there is research to show that the practice of retelling results in improvements in recalling important aspects of the story. Let's look at several examples of rubrics and how they help inform the level of a student's comprehension. (See Appendix pages 187 – 189 for printable copies of the following rubrics.)

Our first example captures features of reading comprehension applicable to both narrative and informational text. This rubric, designed to contrast reading and listening proficiency, can be limited to listening-level text when used with emerging readers. Carreker (2016) explains that "proficient" retelling is measured on this rubric with a preponderance of 3s and 4s. "Not Proficient" retelling is marked by a preponderance of 1s and 2s."

## Retelling Rubric

| Objective | Beginning 1 | Developing 2 | Mastery 3 | Exemplary 4 |
|---|---|---|---|---|
| *Uses complete sentences in retelling the passage* | Uses incomplete sentences—many are not comprehensible | Uses complete and incomplete sentences | Uses complete sentences with simple structure | Uses complete sentences with varied structures |
| *Captures the salient idea of each event* | Does not recall all salient ideas or inaccurately expresses two or more ideas | Expresses one salient idea incompletely or inaccurately | Accurately captures the salient idea of each event but is verbose or not specific enough | Accurately and succinctly captures the salient idea of each event |

| Objective | Beginning 1 | Developing 2 | Mastery 3 | Exemplary 4 |
|---|---|---|---|---|
| *Sequences events cohesively* | Does not include all events or does not state all events in correct order | States events in order but without any transitions | Sequences events using transition words (e.g., *first, then, next, finally*) | Sequences events using words such as, *then, next, therefore, that's why, so, if, because* |
| *Incorporates vocabulary from the passage* | Does not incorporate any vocabulary words from the passage | Incorporates vocabulary words exactly as used in the passage | Uses appropriate synonyms for words from the passage | Uses vocabulary words from the passage in novel ways |
| *Retells the passage with prosody* | Does not complete the retelling and may say "I can't remember" or "I forget" | Restates, pauses, or self-corrects while retelling the passage and may overuse "um" | Retells the passage haltingly but persistently | Retells the passage with ease, confidence, and expression |

Carreker, 2011. Used by permission of Neuhaus Education Center, Bellaire, TX.

The next rubric example aligns with the elements of narrative structure. This rubric rates a student's retelling on the degree to which the student includes the elements of story grammar.

**Retelling Rubric**
**Narrative Text**

| | Beginning 1 | Developing 2 | Proficient 3 |
|---|---|---|---|
| **Setting and Characters** | One main character with a reference to a general place or time and a problem that elicits a character's response, but one that is not directly related to the event | One main character with a specific name and reference(s) to specific places or times and at least one stated event or problem that elicits a character's response | More than one main character with specific names, references to specific places and times, and two or more distinct stated events or problems that elicit the characters' responses |
| **Initiating Event and Actions** | One statement about the character's emotions or feelings but the responses are not related to an event or problem and one statement about how the character might solve the problem; however, the character's actions are not related to the problem itself | One or more statements about the character's emotions or feelings related to an event or problem and two statements about how the character might solve the problem that includes attempts by the character to solve the problem | One or more statements about the character's emotions or feelings related to an event or problem and three or more statements about how the character might solve the problem that includes attempts by the character to solve the problem |

|  | Beginning 1 | Developing 2 | Proficient 3 |
|---|---|---|---|
| Conclusion and Resolution | One statement about what happened at the end of the story | One statement about what happened at the end of the story and how the character(s) felt as a result of the consequence | One statement about what happened at the end of the story including any additional problems/complications that occurred and how the character(s) felt as a result of the consequence |

Based on rubric referenced in Petersen, D.B., Gillam, S.L., & Gillam, R.B. (2008). Emerging Procedures in Narrative Assessment: The Index of Narrative Complexity. *Topics in Language Disorders, 28*, 115-130.

The last example, based on the **Knowledge Tree** activity (See pages 125 – 138), illustrates a rubric designed to rate student performance for retelling informational text that they listen to or read.

## Retelling Rubric for Knowledge Trees
## Informational Text

|  | Beginning 1 | Developing 2 | Proficient 3 |
|---|---|---|---|
| Topic | No topic stated | General statement of topic | Precise label of topic |
| Major subtopic | No subtopics stated | Some subtopics stated | All subtopics stated |
| Supporting details | No supporting details included | Some supporting details included | All or most supporting details included |
| Language Usage | Little or no organization of information from the text selection | Information conveyed using some cohesive ties to show content relationship | Clear use of specific vocabulary and cohesive ties to convey the content information |

In addition to selecting—or creating—rubrics to capture information about what students are learning about the language and content in text, they can be used in two ways—as a recall task or as a language task.

- o Recall task: As a recall task, students retell what they remember from the text selection without using an organizer (e.g., Story Map or Knowledge Tree) as a guide. This format captures both the student's retention of the information and the degree to which the information is communicated clearly.

o   Language task: As a language task, students do the retelling using an organizer as a guide. This format places emphasis on the student's ability to use the structure of the organizer and the use of specific vocabulary from the text selection.

For longitudinal information, it is important to note which format is used and to be consistent across multiple retelling trials.

The use of rubrics can sometimes be a red flag for other issues. Students who have problems with working memory often struggle with retelling. In these cases, it may be appropriate to ask follow-up questions after they have completed the retelling. Questions like the following can prompt students to add to their retelling: "Tell me more about what you have read." "Is there anything else that you want to include?" "Tell me more about what happened." Some children have difficulty with retelling because of expressive language difficulties. Using a graphic organizer with these students may help them organize and express their ideas.

*Using the rubrics*

The following examples of rubric ratings illustrate how different retellings map out against the criteria. Once the features in the rubric are rated (highlighted on rubrics below), the ratings can be transferred to a log, shown below the rubric, for a longitudinal record.

Retelling with narrative text #1:

"A girl went for a walk and she saw a house. And then she fell asleep in a bed. Then the Bears scared her and she ran away."

|  | Beginning 1 | Developing 2 | Proficient 3 |
|---|---|---|---|
| Setting and Characters | One main character with a reference to a general place or time and a problem that elicits a character's response, but one that is not directly related to the event | One main character with a specific name and reference(s) to specific places or times and at least one stated event or problem that elicits a character's response | More than one main character with specific names, references to specific places and times, and two or more distinct stated events or problems that elicit the characters' responses |
| Initiating Event and Actions | One statement about the character's emotions or feelings but the responses are not related to an event or problem and one statement about how the character might solve the problem; however, the character's actions are not related to the problem itself | One or more statements about the character's emotions or feelings related to an event or problem and two statements about how the character might solve the problem that includes attempts by the character to solve the problem | One or more statements about the character's emotions or feelings related to an event or problem and three or more statements about how the character might solve the problem that includes attempts by the character to solve the problem |

|  | Beginning 1 | Developing 2 | Proficient 3 |
|---|---|---|---|
| Conclusion and Resolution | One statement about what happened at the end of the story | One statement about what happened at the end of the story and how the character(s) felt as a result of the consequence | One statement about what happened at the end of the story including any additional problems/complications that occurred and how the character(s) felt as a result of the consequence |

| Date | Text | Setting and Characters | Initiating Event and Actions | Conclusion and Resolution | Total points |
|---|---|---|---|---|---|
| 2/10/20 | Goldilocks and the Three Bears | 1 | 1 | 1 | 3 |
|  |  |  |  |  |  |
|  |  |  |  |  |  |

With three (3) total points, this student demonstrates a "beginning" level of narrative retelling. Instruction needs to focus on helping the student identify precise story grammar elements, such as the name of the characters and specific actions.

Retelling with narrative text #2:

"*Goldilocks and the Three Bears* takes place in the morning when the Bears go out for a walk in the woods. The Bears go for a walk in the woods so their porridge can cool off. Goldilocks is out walking and sees a house and smells something good. She is curious to see what's inside the house. She finds the porridge, chairs to sit on, and beds to sleep in. Then, the Bears return home and find Goldilocks sleeping in Momma's bed. She wakes up and runs from the house."

|  | Beginning 1 | Developing 2 | Proficient 3 |
|---|---|---|---|
| Setting and Characters | One main character with a reference to a general place or time and a problem that elicits a character's response, but one that is not directly related to the event | One main character with a specific name and reference(s) to specific places or times and at least one stated event or problem that elicits a character's response | More than one main character with specific names, references to specific places and times, and two or more distinct stated events or problems that elicit the characters' responses |

|  | Beginning 1 | Developing 2 | Proficient 3 |
|---|---|---|---|
| Initiating Event and Actions | One statement about the character's emotions or feelings but the responses are not related to an event or problem and one statement about how the character might solve the problem; however, the character's actions are not related to the problem itself | One or more statements about the character's emotions or feelings related to an event or problem and two statements about how the character might solve the problem that includes attempts by the character to solve the problem | One or more statements about the character's emotions or feelings related to an event or problem and three or more statements about how the character might solve the problem that includes attempts by the character to solve the problem |
| Conclusion and Resolution | One statement about what happened at the end of the story | One statement about what happened at the end of the story and how the character(s) felt as a result of the consequence | One statement about what happened at the end of the story including any additional problems/complications that occurred and how the character(s) felt as a result of the consequence |

| Date | Text | Setting and Characters | Initiating Event and Actions | Conclusion and Resolution | Total points |
|---|---|---|---|---|---|
| 2/10/20 | Goldilocks and the Three Bears | 2 | 2 | 1 | 5 |
|  |  |  |  |  |  |
|  |  |  |  |  |  |

With five (5) total points, this student's retelling reveals a "developing" level of narrative knowledge for setting and characters and initiating events and actions; however, the student is at a beginning level for consequence and resolution because she didn't mention how Goldilocks felt when the Bears arrived on the scene. Although we can infer that she was upset, and possibly embarrassed, Goldilocks ran out the door and didn't apologize to the Bears for intruding. This indicates that the student needs instruction in the story grammar elements of consequence and resolution.

Retelling with informational text #1

"Things grow in dirt. They have stems and leaves. Wind moves them."

|  | Beginning 1 | Developing 2 | Proficient 3 |
|---|---|---|---|
| Topic | No topic stated | General statement of topic | Precise label of topic |

|  | Beginning 1 | Developing 2 | Proficient 3 |
|---|---|---|---|
| Major subtopic | No subtopics stated | Some subtopics stated | All subtopics stated |
| Supporting details | No supporting details included | Some supporting details included | All or most supporting details included |
| Language Usage | Little or no organization of information from the text selection | Information conveyed using some cohesive ties to show content relationship | Clear use of specific vocabulary and cohesive ties to convey the content information |

| Date | Text | Topic | Major subtopics | Supporting Details | Language Usage | Total points |
|---|---|---|---|---|---|---|
| 2/10/20 | Articles about Plant Seeds and Growth | 1 | 1 | 2 | 1 | 5 |
|  |  |  |  |  |  |  |
|  |  |  |  |  |  |  |

With five (5) points, this student demonstrates a "beginning" level of informational retelling. To distinguish between a recall versus a language issue, instruction could begin by using the completed **Knowledge Tree** organizer as a guide. As the student makes progress more in accurately and completely incorporating vocabulary and information into the retelling, teachers can fade the scaffolding provided by the organizer. For example, the teacher could remove the "leaves" and see to what extent the "trunk" and "branches" help the student retrieve and retell the supporting detail information.

Retelling with informational text #2

> "These articles tell about how seeds grow. They tell about how seeds move. Seeds grow in dirt and they need water and sunlight. That is how we get plants. Seeds move in the wind and some seeds move on animals."

|  | Beginning 1 | Developing 2 | Proficient 3 |
|---|---|---|---|
| Topic | No topic stated | General statement of topic | Precise label of topic |
| Major subtopic | No subtopics stated | Some subtopics stated | All subtopics stated |

|  | Beginning 1 | Developing 2 | Proficient 3 |
|---|---|---|---|
| Supporting details | No supporting details included | Some supporting details included | All or most supporting details included |
| Language Usage | Little or no organization of information from the text selection | Information conveyed using some cohesive ties to show content relationship | Clear use of specific vocabulary and cohesive ties to convey the content information |

| Date | Text | Topic | Major subtopics | Supporting Details | Language Usage | Total points |
|---|---|---|---|---|---|---|
| 2/10/20 | Articles about Plant Seeds and Growth | 2 | 3 | 2 | 2 | 9 |
|  |  |  |  |  |  |  |
|  |  |  |  |  |  |  |

With nine (9) total points, this student demonstrates a "proficient" level of informational retelling. Instruction could focus on incorporating more details into the retelling, as well as using some cohesive ties and sentences that convey the relationship of the information.

Rubrics are generic rather than specific to a text selection. The rubric provides a framework to determine to what extent a student is using and/or incorporating the recurring features of text in their retelling of a selection. Over time, the goal is to see ratings increase as students gain the ability to reflect their understanding of text through their retellings. The ratings can be used to adjust the instructional emphasis. (For practice using the rubrics, see Appendix pages 190 – 197.)

The activities in this domain combine these features of effective instructional practices with emphasis on the big ideas in comprehension:

- Developing narrative knowledge – use story grammar information to select, record, and retell narrative text
- Building background knowledge – focus on selecting and remembering information from expository text to build background knowledge
- Text cohesion – use vocabulary and syntactic clues that connect words and ideas across text
- Inference – use visual clues, verbal clues and background knowledge to develop inference-making skills
- Reading-writing connections – understand the role writing plays in developing reading comprehension and content knowledge

The activities in this domain include:

| | Stage 0 | Stage 1 | Stage 2 |
|---|---|---|---|
| **Instruction** | **Developing Narrative Knowledge (See page 110)** | | |
| | Story Map (Visually represent story elements on a graphic organizer) | Story Map (Visually represent story elements on a graphic organizer) | Story Map (Visually represent story elements on a graphic organizer) |
| | **Building Background Knowledge (See page 125)** | | |
| | Knowledge Trees (Identify information from informational text using predictable text) | Knowledge Trees (Identify information from informational text using code-emphasis text) | Knowledge Trees (Identify information from informational text using authentic text) |
| | **Text Cohesion (See page 139)** | | |
| | Text Links (Use pictures to orally use vocabulary and grammatical connectives) | Text Links (Use decodable text to identify and use vocabulary and grammatical connectives) | Text Links (Use authentic text to identify and use vocabulary and grammatical connectives) |
| | **Inference (See page 146)** | | |
| | What Is It? (Use cues from partial picture to figure out what picture is) | What Is It? (Use cues from partial picture to figure out what picture is) | What Is It? (Use cues from partial picture to figure out what picture is) |
| | Use What You Know (Use background knowledge to expand on picture content) | Use What You Know (Use background knowledge to expand on picture content) | Use What You Know (Use background knowledge to expand on picture content) |
| | **Reading/Writing Connection (See page 159)** | | |
| | Sentence Summaries (Use sentence expansion to integrate writing with use of text information to develop sentences) | Sentence Summaries (Use sentence expansion to integrate writing with use of text information to develop sentences) | Sentence Summaries (Use sentence expansion to integrate writing with use of text information to develop sentences) |
| | What's the Answer? (Use Q/A transformation to generate answers in complete sentences) | What's the Answer? (Use Q/A transformation to generate answers in complete sentences) | What's the Answer? (Use Q/A transformation to generate answers in complete sentences) |

| Stage 0 | Stage 1 | Stage 2 |
|---|---|---|

Assessment

There are two main approaches to assessing understanding of narrative and informational text.

- Answering questions: Open-ended or multiple-choice questions assess students' ability to both recall information from the text and to interpret the questions. (See **What's the Answer?**, pp. 159, 173 - 184)

- Retelling activities: Retellings assess students' ability to use text structure to recall and state text content. (See *Role of retelling rubrics in monitoring student progress in comprehending text*, pages 99 – 102 and Appendix pages 187 – 189 for printable rubrics.)

# Developing Narrative Knowledge

The following set of activities focuses on using story grammar elements to develop narrative knowledge.

**Domain**: Comprehension

**Objective**: To select story grammar information from text to develop narrative knowledge.

**Background information for these activities**:

Teachers can support their students' reading comprehension by making them aware of the structures of different genres – both narrative and informational. In the case of narrative text, this means focusing on the elements of a story—referred to as story grammar—including setting, characters and plot.

Graphic organizers help make abstract concepts concrete. A graphic organizer helps to capture the relevant information and provides students with a structure to remember and retell what they have listened to or read. Graphic organizers can be templates that cue the students for the key information. They can also be generated informally as part of a discussion about a reading selection. Regardless, the purpose is to capture the essential information for future use.

Graphic organizers can also bridge reading and writing by visually representing the specific components of a story. Students capture and organize information while listening to or reading a story for the purpose of retelling the selection. Duke (2014) points out that it is possible (and desirable) to use "...the same or similar graphic organizers to support reading and writing of the same genre." Emphasizing this reciprocity facilitates both comprehension and written expression.

To help students organize information from narrative text, the Story Map activity uses graphic organizers—either a template (see Appendix page 201 – 203) or a graphic that is informally drawn—to provide a visual way to classify information about story grammar—setting, characters, initiating event, reaction/feeling, the plan, actions, consequences, and resolution.

To use the Story Map graphic organizer, students should learn the meaning of each element and to recognize the story content each element conveys. The elements of story grammar are acquired through a developmental progression. The following table depicts an approximation of that acquisition and serves as a guideline for instructional purposes.

| Story Grammar Element[1] | Stage | | |
|---|---|---|---|
| | 0 | 1 | 2 |
| **Setting**: where and when the story takes place | x | x | x |
| **Characters**: the people, animals or creatures who act out the story | x | x | x |
| **Initiating event**: what happens to cause a response that sets a series of other actions in motion. Sometimes referred to as the problem. | | x | x |
| **Reactions/Feelings**: the character's feelings about what happened | x | x | x |
| **The Plan**: what the character plans to do to achieve his/her goals | | | x |

110

| Story Grammar Element[1] | Stage | | |
|---|---|---|---|
| | 0 | 1 | 2 |
| **Actions/Attempts**: the sequence of attempts the character does to carry out the plan. | x | x | x |
| **Consequence**: what happens as a result of the plan and attempts | | x | x |
| **Resolution:** how the character feels about the consequence | | | x |

The following table displays a progression of activities titled Story Map to build story grammar knowledge utilizing stage-specific text[2].

| Stage 0 | Stage 1 | Stage 2 |
|---|---|---|
| With listening-level text<br>• Select and organize story grammar information based on read aloud text | With listening-level text<br>• Select and organize story grammar information based on read aloud text | With authentic text<br>• Select and organize story grammar information from authentic text |

[1]Teachers are encouraged to use a program that explicitly teaches story grammar elements and to adapt this activity using the terminology and graphic supports that are used in that program. (For more information about story grammar elements, see *Elements of story structure*, pages 15 – 16 and *The dynamics that drive a narrative* page 17.)

[2]This activity is described and illustrated using listening-level text for Stages 0 and 1. As students gain ability to read text on their own, they can select and add information from text they read.

# Story Map (Stage 0)

**Objective**: To select story grammar information from text to develop narrative knowledge.

**Target students:** PreK - K

**Materials needed:** Story Map template (see Appendix page 201 for Stage 0 Story Map) with projector or whiteboard/chart paper for hand-drawn template; narrative text selection at students' reading level (i.e., predictable text) or listening level (i.e., approximately 2 years above grade level); sticky notes (3 x 5 size)

**Introductory Lesson:** The introductory lesson is designed to have students distinguish information representative of each story grammar element. Before using the Story Map, spend time teaching each element. (Note: The story grammar elements included in this introductory lesson are those designated for Stage 0 in the table on page 110.) Break the lesson down to focus on one story grammar element (e.g., setting, characters, reactions) at a time. Devote multiple days on each element until students select information from the story that accurately represents that element. (For more information about the story grammar elements, refer to Knowledge for Effective Instruction section pages 15 – 16.)

1.  Tell students that there are important parts to every story. To begin, let's take a look at four parts—**setting, characters, reactions/feelings**, and **actions**.

    - Display the graphic symbol for **setting**. Tell students that the house and tree are to remind us that the setting tells the when (time) and where (place) the narrative takes place.

        Read the beginning of a story to students and guide them in identifying the setting. For example, in *Goldilocks and the Three Bears*, the time is the morning when the bears go out for a walk; the place is the woods and the bears' house where Goldilocks stops for a visit. Record the "when" and "where" on separate sticky notes.

        Continue to read other stories to students to illustrate various examples of "where" and "when" (e.g., for when: once upon a time, late last night, on Halloween; for where: in a faraway land, in the barnyard, around the neighborhood). Select stories that have a very clear setting so that you can build your students' schema for a variety of settings. Continue to record each example of "where" and "when." Use a variety of stories and movies, both familiar and unfamiliar, providing practice so the students learn to identify each element. Save the sticky notes for future practice and review.

    - Display the graphic symbol for **characters**. Tell students that the figures of people and the dog are to remind us that characters are the people, animals or individuals who act out the events in the story.

        Read a story to your students and help them identify the characters. In *Goldilocks and the Three Bears*, the characters are Pappa Bear, Momma Bear, Baby Bear, and Goldilocks.

        Explain to students that characters can be real people and animals or they can be imaginary, like Sponge Bob Square Pants. Emphasize with students that usually there are main characters who act out the key events. Record the characters on separate sticky notes. Use a variety of stories and movies to guide students in identifying these important characters. Save the sticky notes for future practice and review.

- ☺ ☹  Display the graphic symbol for **reactions/feelings**. Explain to students that the faces are to remind us that characters react to events in the story and have different feelings throughout the story.

> Read a story to your students and help them identify the feelings of the main characters. In *Goldilocks and the Three Bears*, Goldilocks sees a house in the woods and smells something good to eat. She is curious to see what's inside the house. (She's also very hungry!) Later in the story, the Three Bears are surprised to find Goldilocks asleep in Momma's bed. Record the characters' feelings and reactions on sticky notes.

> Use a variety of stories where the characters exhibit a range of emotions so that the children learn to identify this element in different stories. Save the sticky notes for future practice and review.

☐ ➡ ☐ ➡ ☐  • Display the graphic symbol for **actions**. Explain to students that a story is made up of a sequence of actions from the beginning to the end. Explain that we figure out the actions by asking questions such as: What happened first? Then what happened? What happened next?[1]

> Read a story to students. Tell them to listen for actions—things that characters do—that tell the important events in a story. Guide the students to identify the major actions. For example, in *Goldilocks and the Three Bears,* a sequence of major actions is:
> - The Bear Family goes for a walk in the woods while their porridge cools.
> - Goldilocks comes to the Bear Family's empty house and finds porridge to taste, chairs to sit on, and beds to sleep in.
> - The Bear family returns to find Goldilocks sleeping in Momma's bed.
> - Goldilocks wakes up and runs from the house.
>
> Record each action in the story on a separate sticky note.

> Practice this story grammar element with students to help them focus on the main actions. Read a variety of stories—both familiar and unfamiliar—to ensure that they can identify each story grammar element. Save the sticky notes for future practice and review.[2]

**How to do this activity:**

1. After completing the introductory lessons, display the Story Map graphic organizer for Stage 0. Tell students that the Story Map helps organize what they hear or read in a story. Describe the parts of the organizer. Review with students what each part of the organizer represents:

    a. The **setting** is where and when the story takes place.

    b. **Characters** are the people, animals or creatures who act out the story.

    c. **Reactions/feelings:** the character's feelings about what happened.

    d. **Actions** are the sequence of actions the character does in a story.

Story Map

2. Have students listen to or read the narrative text (i.e., story)[3]. Using the order of information on the graphic organizer, ask students to tell information from the story. Write what they recall on individual sticky notes. Place the notes on the Story Map.

3. After the information is placed on the Story Map, read each sticky note with students.

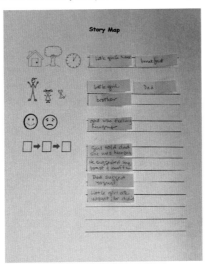

4. Finally, use the graphic organizer to retell the story. Model how to start with the sticky note on the setting and progress through the remaining elements on the organizer. For example

> "This story takes place at breakfast time in the little girl's kitchen. She tells her dad that she is feeling hungry. He suggests she eat soup, toast, or a muffin. The little girl doesn't eat them because her brother ate them. Then her dad suggests yogurt. The little girl eats the yogurt because her brother hadn't eaten yogurt."

5. Have several students take turns retelling the story using the information on the Story Map as a guide.

**Tips for Teaching**:

[1]Sentence frames can be useful to help students retell the sequence of actions or events. For example:

First _____. Then _____. Finally _____.

As students' language proficiency grows, the frames can more closely align with the language of stories, such as:

Once upon a time _____. Suddenly _____. Then _____.
In the end _____.

[2]An effective way to review the story grammar elements is to sort the saved sticky notes into the correct story grammar element categories. The goal of the sort is to recognize the kind of information that represents each story grammar element.

Read a sticky note to the students and have them decide which element the information represents.

| | | | |
|---|---|---|---|
| in the morning | Momma Bear | curious | Bear family goes for a walk in the woods |
| once upon a time | Pappa Bear | upset | Goldilocks finds Bear's empty house |
| in the woods | Baby Bear | frightened | Goldilocks tastes porridge |
| at the Bears' house | Goldilocks | surprised | Goldilocks tries sitting in chairs |
| | | confused | Goldilocks tries beds and falls asleep |
| | | | Bears return and find Goldilocks in bed. |
| | | | Goldilocks wakes up and runs from the house |

[3]This lesson is based on the poem *The Hungry Girl* from www.ReadWorks.org.

## Story Map (Stage 1)

**Objective**: To select story grammar information from text to develop narrative knowledge.

**Target students:** 1

**Materials needed:** Story Map template (see Appendix page 202 for Stage 1 Story Map) with project or whiteboard/chart paper for hand-drawn template; narrative text selection at students' reading level (i.e., decodable text) or listening level (i.e., approximately 2 years above grade level); sticky notes (3 x 5 size)

**Introductory Lesson:** The introductory lesson is designed to have students distinguish information representative of each story grammar element. Before using the Story Map, spend time teaching each story grammar element. (Note: The story grammar elements included in this introductory lesson are those designated for Stage 1 in the table on page 110.) Break the lesson down to focus on one story grammar element (e.g., setting, characters, reactions) at a time. Devote multiple days on each element until students select information from the story that accurately represents that element. (For more information about the story grammar elements, refer to Knowledge for Effective Instruction section pages 15 – 16.)

1. Tell students that there are important parts to every story. To begin, let's take a look at six parts—**setting, characters, initiating event, reactions/feelings, actions/attempts,** and **consequence**.

   - | Setting |
     
     Highlight the part of the Story Map graphic organizer for **setting**. Tell students that the house and tree are to remind us that the setting tells the when (time) and where (place) the narrative takes place.

     Read the beginning of a story to students and guide them in identifying the setting. For example, in *Goldilocks and the Three Bears*, the time is the morning when the bears go out for a walk; the place is the woods and the bears' house where Goldilocks stops for a visit. Record the "when" and "where" on separate sticky notes.

     Continue to read other stories to students to illustrate various examples of "where" and "when" (e.g., for when: once upon a time, late last night, on Halloween; for where: in a faraway land, in the barnyard, around the neighborhood). Select stories that have a very clear setting so that you can build your students' schema for a variety of settings. Continue to record each example of "where" and "when." Use a variety of stories and movies, both familiar and unfamiliar, providing practice so the students learn to identify each element. Save the sticky notes for future practice and review.

   - | Character |
     
     Highlight the part of the Story Map graphic organizer for **characters**. Tell students that the figures of people and the dog are to remind us that characters are the people, animals or individuals who act out the events in the story.

     Read a story to your students and help them identify the characters. In *Goldilocks and the Three Bears*, the characters are Pappa Bear, Momma Bear, Baby Bear, and Goldilocks. Explain to students that characters can be real people and animals or they can be imaginary, like Sponge Bob Square Pants.

Emphasize with students that usually there are main characters who act out the key events. Record the characters on separate sticky notes. Use a variety of stories and movies to guide students in identifying these important characters. Save the sticky notes for future practice and review.

- [ Initiating Event ] Highlight the part of the Story Map graphic organizer for **initiating event**. Explain that this event is something that happens that sets a series of actions in motion. Often this is referred to as the problem.

> In *Goldilocks and the Three Bears*, a very hungry Goldilocks smells porridge and sees it cooling on the windowsill of a little cottage.

Use a variety of stories and movies that are familiar to the students to provide more examples of an initiating event. Be sure to illustrate how positive events can be an initiating event, such as winning a prize.

- [ Reaction/Feelings ] Highlight the part of the Story Map graphic organizer for **reaction/feeling**. Explain to students that the faces are to remind us that characters react to events in the story and have different feelings throughout the story.

> Read a story to your students and help them identify the feelings of the main characters. In *Goldilocks and the Three Bears*, Goldilocks sees a cottage in the woods and smells something good to eat. She is curious to see what's inside the house. Later in the story, the Three Bears are surprised to find Goldilocks asleep in Momma's bed. Record the characters' feelings and reactions on sticky notes.

Use a variety of stories where the characters exhibit a range of emotions so that the children learn to identify this element in different stories. Save the sticky notes for future practice and review.

- [ Actions/Attempts ] Highlight the part of the Story Map for **actions**. Explain to students that a story is made up of a sequence of actions from the beginning to the end. Explain that we figure out the actions by asking questions such as: What happened first? Then what happened? What happened next?

> Read a story to students. Tell them to listen for actions—things that characters do—that tell the important event in a story. Guide the students to identify the major actions. For example, in *Goldilocks and the Three Bears,* a sequence of major actions is:
> - Goldilocks walks into the Bear family's empty cottage and tastes the porridge.
> - It's too hot to eat so she explores the other rooms in the cottage while the porridge cools.
> - Goldilocks falls asleep in Momma Bear's bed.
> - When Goldilocks wakes up, she is frightened to see the Three Bears staring at her and runs from the house.
>
> Record each action in the story on a separate sticky note.

Practice this story grammar element with students to help them focus on the main actions. Read a variety of stories—both familiar and unfamiliar—to ensure that they can identify each story grammar element. Save the sticky notes for future practice and review.[1]

- | Consequence |
  |---|

  Highlight the part of the Story Map graphic organizer for **consequence**. Explain that near the end of the story, we find out how the character's plan turns out.

> In *Goldilocks and the Three Bears*, Goldilocks plan is to eat the porridge that she sees and smells. While she's waiting for it to cool off so that she can eat it, she falls asleep in Momma Bear's bed. When the Three Bears find her, she is surprised and afraid so she runs out of their cottage.
>
> Like this familiar story, many stories have complicated endings.
>
> Use other stories to provide students with practice identifying this element in a story. Ask students the question: *How did the character's plan work out?*

**How to do this activity:**

1.  Display the Story Map graphic organizer. Tell students that the Story Map helps organize what they listen to or read in a story. Describe the parts of the organizer. Review with students what each part of the organizer represents:

    a.  The **setting** is where and when the story takes place.

    b.  **Characters** are the people, animals or creatures who act out the story.

    c.  An **initiating event** is an action or event that sets the story in motion. Often, but not always, an initiating event is a problem that needs to be solved.

    d.  **Reactions/feelings** are the characters' feelings about what happened.

    e.  **Actions/Attempts** are the sequence of attempts the character does to carry out the plan.

    f.  **Consequence** tells what happens as a result of the plan and attempts.

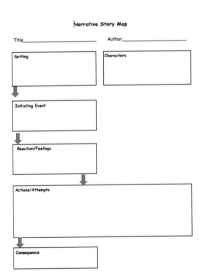

2. Have students listen to or read the narrative text (i.e., story)[1]. Using the order of information on the graphic organizer, ask students to tell information from the story. Write what they recall on individual sticky notes.[2] Place the notes on the Story Map.

3. After the information is placed on the Story Map, read each sticky note with students.

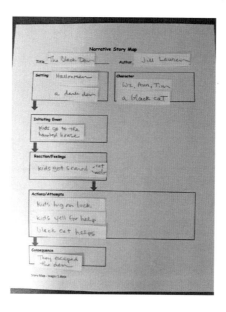

4. Finally, use the graphic organizer to retell the story. Model how to start with the sticky notes for the setting and progress through the remaining elements on the organizer. For example:

> "This story takes place on Halloween at a haunted house called the black den. Liz, Ann, and Tim went into the den, which was a haunted house, and got scared by a rat and a web. They wanted to leave but couldn't get out. They tugged on the lock, yelled for help, and got help from a black cat who had special power to get them out. Finally, the kids escaped the den."

5. Have several students take turns retelling the story using the information on the Story Map as a guide.

**Tips for Teaching:**

[1]This lesson is based on the decodable story *In the Den* from Jill Lauren www.whole-phonics.com.

[2]Sticky notes are recommended in the initial stages of learning to complete the story map. The sticky notes allow for easy additions and changes to the map without having to rewrite information. As students gain proficiency in identifying story grammar elements when they read, they can transition to writing the information directly on the graphic organizer.

## Story Map (Stage 2)

**Objective**: To select story grammar information from text to develop narrative knowledge.

**Target students:** 2 – 3

**Materials needed:** Story Map template (see Appendix page 203 for Stage 2 Story Map) with project or whiteboard/chart paper for hand-drawn template; narrative text selection at students' reading level (i.e., authentic text) or listening level (i.e., approximately 2 years above grade level); sticky notes (3 x 5 size)

**Introductory Lesson:** The introductory lesson is designed to have students distinguish information representative of each story grammar element. Before using the Story Map, spend time teaching each story grammar element. (Note: The story grammar elements included in this introductory lesson are those designated for Stage 2 in the table on page 110.) Break the lesson down to focus on each story grammar element (e.g., setting, characters, reactions) at a time. Devote multiple days on one element until students select information from the story that accurately represents that element. (For more information about the story grammar elements, refer to Knowledge for Effective Instruction section pages 15 – 16.)

1. Tell students that there are important parts to every story. To begin, let's take a look at seven parts—**setting, characters, initiating event, reactions/feelings, plan, actions/attempts,** and **consequence/resolution**.

   - Highlight the part of the Story Map graphic organizer for **setting**. Tell students that the house and tree are to remind us that the setting tells the when (time) and where (place) the narrative takes place.

     Read the beginning of a story to students and guide them in identifying the setting. For example, in *Goldilocks and the Three Bears*, the time is the morning when the bears go out for a walk; the place is the woods and the bears' house where Goldilocks stops for a visit. Record the "when" and "where" on separate sticky notes.

     Continue to read other stories to students to illustrate various examples of "where" and "when" (e.g., for when: once upon a time, late last night, on Halloween; for where: in a faraway land, in the barnyard, around the neighborhood). Select stories that have a very clear setting so that you can build your students' schema for a variety of settings. Continue to record each example of "where" and "when." Use a variety of stories and movies, both familiar and unfamiliar, providing practice so the students learn to identify each element. Save the sticky notes for future practice and review.

   - Highlight the part of the Story Map graphic organizer for **characters**. Tell students that the figures of people and the dog are to remind us that characters are the people, animals or individuals who act out the events in the story.

     Read a story to your students and help them identify the characters. In *Goldilocks and the Three Bears*, the characters are Pappa Bear, Momma Bear, Baby Bear, and Goldilocks. Explain to students that characters can be real people and animals or they can be imaginary, like Sponge Bob Square Pants.

120

Emphasize with students that usually there are main characters who act out the key events. Record the characters on separate sticky notes. Use a variety of stories and movies to guide students in identifying these important characters. Save the sticky notes for future practice and review.

- | Initiating Event |
  Highlight the part of the Story Map graphic organizer for **initiating event**. Explain that this event is something that happens that sets a series of actions in motion. Often this is referred to as the problem.

    In *Goldilocks and the Three Bears*, a very hungry Goldilocks smells porridge and sees it cooling on the windowsill of a little cottage.

    Use a variety of stories and movies that are familiar to the students to provide more examples of an initiating event. Be sure to illustrate how positive events can be an initiating event, such as winning a prize.

- | Reaction/Feelings |
  Highlight the part of the Story Map graphic organizer for **reaction/feeling**. Explain to students that the faces are to remind us that characters react to events in the story and have different feelings throughout the story.

    Read a story to your students and help them identify the feelings of the main characters. In *Goldilocks and the Three Bears*, Goldilocks is really hungry and curious to see what the porridge tastes like. Record the characters' feelings and reactions on sticky notes.

    Use a variety of stories where the characters exhibit a range of emotions so that the children learn to identify this element in different stories. Save the sticky notes for future practice and review.

- | The Plan |
  Highlight the part of the Story Map graphic organizer for the **plan**. Explain that this is what the characters do to achieve their goals.

    In the case of *Goldilocks and the Three Bears*, Goldilocks decides to taste the porridge and explores the rest of the cottage while the porridge cools.

- | Actions/Attempts |
  Highlight the part of the Story Map graphic organizer for **actions**. Explain to students that a story is made up of a sequence of actions from beginning to the end. Explain that we figure out the actions by asking questions such as: What happened first? Then what happened? What happened next?

    Read a story to students. Tell them to listen for actions—things that characters do—that tell the important event in a story. Guide the students to identify the major actions. For example, in *Goldilocks and the Three Bears*, a sequence of major actions is:
    - Goldilocks walks into the Bear family's empty cottage and tastes the porridge.

- It's too hot to eat so she explores the other rooms in the cottage while the porridge cools.
- Goldilocks falls asleep in Momma Bear's bed.
- When Goldilocks wakes up, she is frightened to see the Three Bears staring at her and runs from the house.

Record each action in the story on a separate sticky note.

Practice this story grammar element with students to help them focus on the main actions. Read a variety of stories—both familiar and unfamiliar—to ensure that they can identify each story grammar element. Save the sticky notes for future practice and review.[1]

```
┌─────────────────────────┐
│ Consequence             │
│                         │
│                         │
└─────────────────────────┘
```
Highlight the part of the Story Map graphic organizer for **consequence.** Explain that near the end of the story, we find out how the character's plan turns out.

In *Goldilocks and the Three Bears*, Goldilocks plan is to eat the porridge that she sees and smells. While she's waiting for it to cool off so that she can eat it, she falls asleep in Momma Bear's bed and when the Three Bears find her, she is surprised and afraid so she runs out of their cottage. Like this familiar story, many stories have complicated endings.

```
┌─────────────────────────┐
│ Resolution              │
│                         │
│                         │
└─────────────────────────┘
```
Highlight the part of the Story Map graphic organizer for **resolution.** Explain that the characters in stories usually experience different feelings during the story.

In the beginning of the story, Goldilocks is both hungry and curious and decides to try the porridge she smells and sees. However, at the end of the story, when she sees how surprised and upset the Three Bears are to find that she has broken into their home, she is frightened and feels sorry for what she did. This is called the resolution and it tells how the character feels about how their plan worked out. Sometimes this part of the story is also called the theme or lesson.

Be sure to use other stories to provide students with practice identifying this element in a story. Ask students the question: *How did the character feel at the end of the story? How was this feeling different than how s/he felt when the kick-off occurred?*

Use other stories to provide students with practice identifying this element in a story. Ask students the question: *How did the character's plan work out?*

**How to do this activity:**

1. Display the Story Map graphic organizer. Tell students that the Story Map helps organize what they listen to or read in a story. Describe the parts of the organizer. Review with students what each part of the organizer represents:

   a. The **setting** is where and when the story takes place.

   b. **Characters** are the people, animals or creatures who act out the story.

c. **Initiating event**, sometimes referred to as the problem, tells what happens to cause a response that sets a series of other actions in motion.

d. **Reactions/Feeling**: the character's feelings about what happened

e. **The Plan**: what the character plans to do to achieve his/her goals

f. **Actions/Attempts** are the sequence of attempts the character does to carry out the plan.

g. **Consequence** tells what happens as a result of the plan and attempts.

h. **Resolution:** how the character feels about the consequence

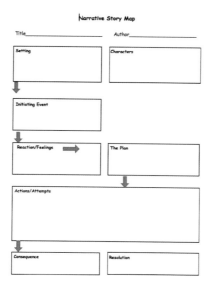

2. Have students listen to or read the narrative text (i.e., story).[2] Using the order of information on the graphic organizer, ask students to tell information from the story. Write what they recall on individual sticky notes. Place the notes on the Story Map.

3. After the information is placed on the Story Map, read each sticky note with students.

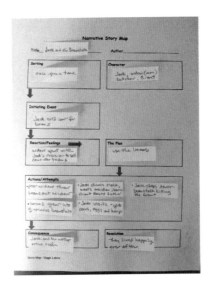

4. Finally, use the graphic organizer to retell the story. Model how to start with the sticky notes for the setting and progress through the remaining elements on the organizer. For example:

> "Jack and the Beanstalk takes place long ago in a make-believe world ('once upon a time'). Jack and his widow mother were poor so they couldn't buy things that they needed. Jack's mother was worried about feeding her son, so she decided she had to sell their cow to get money for food. Jack sold the cow for beans. The poor widow was upset with Jack's decision and threw the beans out the window. They grew into a ginormous beanstalk. Jack climbed to the top and met a maiden who told him that the giant in the castle at the top of the stalk had slain Jack's father. While the giant slept, Jack stole his coins. The next visit, Jack stole the hen who laid golden eggs. On the next visit, Jack stole the magic harp. The giant woke up and started to chase Jack. Jack was faster and got down the beanstalk and chopped it down, which made the giant fall to his death. Jack and his mother were very rich and lived happily ever after."

5. Have several students take turns retelling the story using the information on the Story Map as a guide.

**Tips for Teaching**:

[1]Sticky notes are recommended in the initial stages of learning to complete the story map. The sticky notes allow for easy additions and changes to the map without having to rewrite information. As students gain proficiency in identifying story grammar elements when they read, they can transition to writing the information directly on the graphic organizer.

[2]This lesson is based on the authentic text *Jack and the Beanstalk* from www.ReadWorks.org.

## Building Background Knowledge

The following activity set focuses on selecting and remembering information from text to build background knowledge

**Domain**: Comprehension

**Objective**: To select information from text to build background knowledge.

**Background information for these activities**:

Background knowledge is foundational for all aspects of literacy development but particularly for its role in comprehension. Background knowledge and reading comprehension are interdependent: one is necessary to build the other. Given the importance of growing students' background knowledge, teachers must model for children how to select, organize, and remember content information.

In the case of expository text, an integral part of this selection process is understanding that information can be categorized based on meaning. Such classification—through the development of semantic networks—also facilitates recall. Additionally, through the classification (i.e., sorting) process, students increase their awareness of the hierarchy of information (e.g., main ideas and supporting details). When the classified content is supplemented by information from multiple sources on the same topic, students expand their knowledge by gradually adding to what they already know. (Wright, 2019)

The following table displays a progression of background knowledge building activities utilizing stage-specific text[1].

| Stage 0 | Stage 1 | Stage 2 |
|---|---|---|
| With listening-level text<br>• Select and organize content associations based on read aloud text | With listening-level text<br>• Select and organize content associations based on read aloud text | With authentic text<br>• Select and organize content associations from authentic text that students read |

[1]This activity is described and illustrated using listening-level text for Stages 0 and 1. As students gain ability to read text on their own, they can select and add information from sources they read.

**How to do the activity:**

The Knowledge Trees activity helps students organize content information from informational text. The graphic organizer—either a template (see Appendix page 204) or a graphic that is informally drawn—provides a visual way to classify information about a topic, subtopics, and details. Additionally, multiple sources of information on the same topic adds to the students' knowledge (i.e., more leaves on the trees) in a gradual and cumulative way.

The Knowledge Trees activity follows these basic steps:

1. Display the Knowledge Tree graphic organizer. Tell students that the Knowledge Tree helps them organize what they listen to or read. Describe the parts of the organizer. Tell students
    a. The trunk is where we write the **topic**. The topic is what the whole article is about.

b. The branches are where we write **subtopics**. Subtopics are categories of information about the topic.

c. The leaves are where we write **details**. The details provide information about the subtopics. Details are often descriptive.

 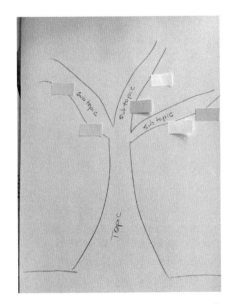

Note: The different color sticky notes illustrate information from multiple articles. Yellow notes are from the first article students listen to, pink notes are from a second article, and the green are from a third selection.

2. Read the article to students.[1] Ask students to tell information they heard in the article. Write what they recall on individual sticky notes.[2]

3. After students recall as many pieces of information as they can, read each sticky note to students and decide if it is the topic, subtopic or detail. Model the thinking involved in deciding where each piece of information belongs. Place the notes on the Knowledge Tree accordingly.

4. When all of the sticky notes are placed on the Knowledge Tree, use the graphic organizer to summarize the content.

5. In subsequent lessons, read additional articles on the same topic to students. Have students listen for more subtopics and details to add to the Knowledge Tree. Repeat the process of writing sticky notes to record the information that students recall. Again, place the additional notes on the Knowledge Tree.

[1] As students are able to read the text themselves, they can select and add information from sources they read.

[2] Initially, the teacher should be the scribe for the information students recall. As students learn transcription skills (i.e., writing and spelling), they can do their own recording.

## Knowledge Trees (Stage 0)

**Objective**: To select information from text to build background knowledge.

**Target students:** PreK - K

**Materials needed:** Knowledge Tree template with project or whiteboard/chart paper for hand-drawn template; several informational text selections on the same topic at students' listening level[1] (i.e., approximately 2 years above grade level); sticky notes (3 x 5 size); prepared sticky notes for the topic and subtopics for the selections[2]

**How to do this activity:**
1. Display the Knowledge Tree graphic organizer. Tell students that the Knowledge Tree helps organize what they listen to or read. Describe the parts of the organizer. Tell students

    a. The trunk is where we write the **topic**. The topic is what the whole article is about.

    b. The branches are where we write **subtopics**. The branches are categories of information about the topic.

    c. The leaves are where we write **details**. The details provide information about the subtopics. Details are often descriptive.

2. Place the prepared sticky note for the topic on trunk (healthy diet). Tell students that the whole article will be about this topic.

3. Next, add the prepared sticky notes for the subtopics (fruits and vegetables, whole grains, meats and beans, and dairy foods) on the branches. Tell students that these are categories about the topic.

4. Read the article to students and ask them to listen for information about the subtopics—fruits and vegetables, whole grains, meats and beans, and dairy foods. While reading the selection to the students, ask them to tell information they heard in the article. Write what they recall on individual sticky notes.[2] Display the sticky notes as you write them.

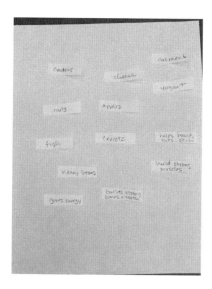

5.  After students recall as many pieces of information as they can, read each sticky note to students and decide where (i.e., which branch (subtopic)) each piece of information fits. Model the thinking involved in deciding which category a piece of information fits into. Place each note on the Knowledge Tree according to its category.

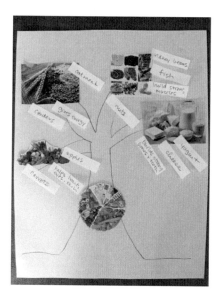

6.  After all of the pieces of information are placed on the tree, use the graphic organizer to summarize the content. Model how to start with the sticky note on the trunk and then add a branch and details to create an oral summary. For example:

> "This article is about having a healthy diet. Some healthy foods are fruits and vegetables. They help our heart, eyes, and skin. Carrots and apples are kinds of foods in this group. Whole grains

give us energy. Crackers and oatmeal are in this group. Meats and beans help us build strong muscles. Fish, nuts, and kidney beans are examples. Dairy foods build strong bones and teeth. Cheese and yogurt are kinds of dairy foods."

Have several students take turns saying a summary of the information.

7. Read other articles to students on the same topic.[3] Write sticky notes with information—subtopics and details—that students recall from the new article. Add the additional notes to the Knowledge Tree to build content knowledge for the topic.

**Tips for Teaching**:

[1]This lesson is based on the article *Eat Right Feel Great* from a grade 2 Article-A-Day article set from www.ReadWorks.org.

[2]Notes may be in the form of drawings or illustrations for kindergarteners and some first graders.

[3]Additional articles can be read on subsequent days. Distributing content learning over a period of time helps to cumulatively build content-specific knowledge.

## Knowledge Trees (Stage 1)

**Objective**: To select information from text to build background knowledge.

**Target students:** 1

**Materials needed:** Knowledge Tree template with project or whiteboard/chart paper for hand-drawn template; several informational text selections on the same topic at students' listening level[1] (i.e., approximately 2 years above grade level); sticky notes (3 x 5 size); prepared sticky notes for the topic for the selection

**How to do this activity:**
1. Display the Knowledge Tree graphic organizer. Tell students that the Knowledge Tree helps organize what they listen to or read. Describe the parts of the organizer. Tell students

   a. The trunk is where we write the **topic**. The topic is what the whole article is about.

   b. The branches are where we write **subtopics**. The branches are categories of information about the topic.

   c. The leaves are where we write **details**. The details provide information about the subtopics. Details are often descriptive.

2. Place the prepared sticky note for the topic on trunk (celebrations around the world). Tell students that the whole article will be about this topic.

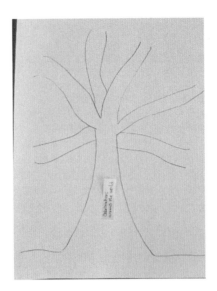

3. While reading the article to students, ask them to listen for information about the topic. Write what they identify on individual sticky notes. Display the sticky notes as you write them.

4. After students identify as many pieces of information as they can, read each sticky note to students and guide them to identify the subtopics.[2] For example, you could ask students what places around the world have celebrations mentioned in the selection (i.e., the countries—Peru, Bulgaria, Ghana, Australia, China, and the United States). Place these sticky notes on the branches of the Knowledge Tree. Draw more branches as needed.

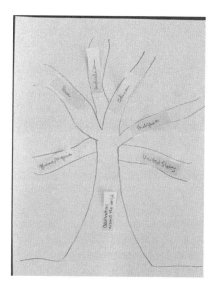

5.  Next guide students in deciding which category a piece of information fits into.[2] Place each note on the Knowledge Tree according to its category. Reread parts of the selection as needed.

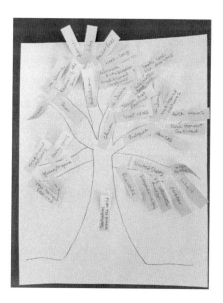

6.  After all of the pieces of information are placed on the tree, use the graphic organizer to summarize the content. Model how to start with the sticky note on the trunk and then add a branch and details to create an oral summary. For example:

    "This article is about celebrations around the world. Peru celebrates the sun in a Festival of the Sun. In Bulgaria, people celebrate roses with folk music and dances. Ghana and Nigeria have a celebration for yams in August. In July, people in Australia celebrate Aborigines. The Dragon Boat Festival takes place in China to celebrate good luck. In the United States, people celebrate their freedom on July 4th. People wear red, white and blue, march in parades and watch fireworks."

Have several students take turns saying a summary.[3]

7. Read other articles to students on the same topic.[4] Write sticky notes with information—subtopics and details—that students recall from the new article. Add the additional notes to the Knowledge Tree to build content knowledge for the topic.

**Tips for Teaching:**

[1]This lesson is based on the article *Celebrations Around the World* from a grade 3 Article-A-Day article set from www.ReadWorks.org.

[2]Initially, select the sticky notes for the subtopics to place on the Knowledge Tree for the students. Explain why these are the categories of information for the article. Continue to model this process for students to increase their awareness of how to create categories of information and to sort the details into those categories.

[3]The information on the Knowledge Tree can also be used for the **Sentence Summaries** activity (see pages 163 – 164, 167 – 168, 171 – 172).

[4]Additional articles can be read on subsequent days. Distributing content learning over a period of time helps to cumulatively build content-specific knowledge.

## Knowledge Trees (Stage 2)

**Objective**: To select information from text selections to build background knowledge.

**Target students:** 2 – 3

**Materials needed:** Knowledge Tree template with project or whiteboard/chart paper for hand-drawn template; several informational text selections on the same topic at students' reading level[1]; sticky notes (3 x 5 size); prepared sticky note for the topic

**How to do this activity:**

1. Display the Knowledge Tree graphic organizer. Tell students that the Knowledge Tree helps organize what they read. Describe the parts of the organizer. Tell students

   d. The trunk is where we write the **topic**. The topic is what a whole article or several related articles are about.

   e. The branches are where we write **subtopics**. The branches are categories of information about the topic.

   f. The leaves are where we write **details**. The details provide information about the subtopics. Details are often descriptive.

2. Place the prepared sticky note for the topic on trunk (seeds). Tell students that the articles they are going to read about this topic.

3. Have students read the first article about the seeds.[1] Provide students with sticky notes and ask them to write one piece of information from the article. Have students read their sticky note and display it on a large piece of chart paper. If students duplicate information, combine the two on the chart paper.

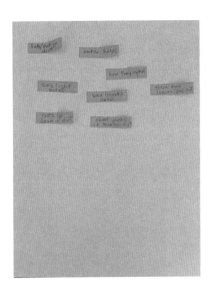

4. After students identify and record as much information as they can, read all of the sticky notes with the students. Guide them to identify the subtopics (i.e., categories). For example, you could ask students what is one big idea we read about seeds in the selection (e.g., how they grow). Find a sticky note with the category among those posted on the chart paper. If there isn't one stating the category, write it and place these it on a branch of the Knowledge Tree. Repeat until students identify the subtopics among the sticky notes for the article.

5.  Place each sticky note on the Knowledge Tree according to its category. Encourage students to refer to and reread parts of the selection as needed to find evidence in the text.

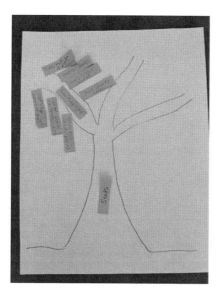

6.  Have students read another article on the same topic. Repeat the process of having students write sticky notes with additional information about the topic. When reviewing the sticky notes, help students determine if they have a new subtopic (branch) to label on the tree (e.g., how they move). Add the sticky note to the branch along with the details. While not essential, it may be helpful to use a different color sticky note for each article to show that the source of the information is different.

 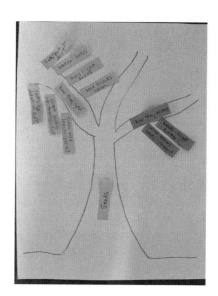

7. Continue to have students read articles on the same topic and add information to the Knowledge Tree.

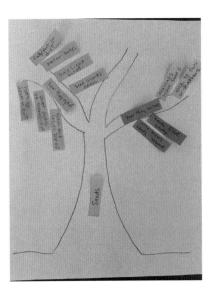

8. After all of the pieces of information are placed on the tree, use the graphic organizer to summarize the content. Model how to start with the sticky note on the trunk and then add each branch and details to create an oral summary. For example:

> "These articles are about how seeds grow and move. Seeds grow when they fall into dirt. Then they need water and sunlight to break open. Roots go down into the dirt. Shoots push up through the dirt. Stems and leaves pop out to make a plant. Some seeds float away when the wind blows. Other seeds move on animals' fur or feather."

Have several students take turns saying a summary of the information. [3]

**Tips for Teaching**:

[1]This lesson is based on articles from the *Plant Seeds and Growth* Article-A-Day article set for grade 2 from www.ReadWorks.org. The first set of information sticky notes (pink) is from *How Do Seeds Grow?*. The second set of information sticky notes (blue) is from *Wind Helps Plants Grow*. The third set of notes (green) is from *Seeds Need to Move*.

[2]An alternative approach is to have small groups of students read different articles on the same topic. During the steps for gathering information, students will draw upon the information in the particular article their group read.

[3]The information on the Knowledge Tree can also be used for the **Sentence Summaries** activity (see pages 163 – 164, 167 – 168, 171 – 172).

# Text Cohesion

The following set of activities focuses on developing awareness of cohesion in text through the use of referential connectives.[1]

**Domain**: Comprehension

**Objective**: To use vocabulary and syntactic clues that connect words and ideas across text.

**Background information for these activities**:

Skilled readers strive to build coherence in order to understand what a text is trying to communicate (Beck & McKeown, 1981, 1986). In order to build coherence, the reader must process the relationships between and among the words in the text. The interpretation and use of connectives when reading is crucial to the construction of a coherent situation model of a text, the hallmark of successful comprehension (Cain & Nash, 2011).

Attention to cross-text referential connectives is a starting point for students to monitor their comprehension about text. These connectives are what Schleppegrell refers to as chains of references (2013). She explains, "Taking time to identify and relate the words and phrases through which these chains are developed helps students gain insight into both the content of what they are reading and how the language resources work." These two types of meaning connectives are foundational to understanding how content and ideas link across sentences in text. Recognizing how synonyms maintain the topic throughout the text is key to grasping the overarching meaning of text. Similarly, identifying pronouns in text and being able to "translate" pronouns into their antecedents is a first step in comprehension monitoring.

| Stage 0 | Stage 1 | Stage 2 |
|---|---|---|
| Using pictures and listening level text <br> • Describe picture content using pronoun referents and synonymous vocabulary | Using code-emphasis (decodable) and listening-level text <br> • Identify pronoun referents and synonymous vocabulary to understand the text | Using authentic text at both reading and listening level text <br> • Identify pronoun referents and synonymous vocabulary to comprehend the topic of text |

[1]Writers use other types of cohesive devices than referential (e.g., pronoun referents and synonyms) to build and connect meaning in text. These other connectives, referred to by McNamara and others as deep cohesion, signal the organization and idea connections across sentences and paragraphs. For example, **a long time ago…the next day** signals time sequence. The words **but…because** signal a causal relationship. We have focused this activity on referential connectives because they are more explicit for beginning readers and as such, they are easier to identify while reading – one of the first steps in monitoring their own comprehension.

**Text Links (Stage 0)**

**Objective**: To use vocabulary and syntactic clues that connect content and ideas across text.

**Target students**: PreK – K

**Materials needed**: Photos or pictures of people, places and things[1]

**How to do the activity**:

1. Review with students that there are words that we use instead of our real names or the name for the object. These words are called pronouns[2]. We use them instead of namers. For example, instead of saying "**Carlos** sat on the chair.", we could say "**He** sat on the chair." The word **he** is a pronoun that refers to **Carlos**. (Provide other examples). We also can refer to a namer using other words that mean the same thing. These are called synonyms. For example, instead of saying "**Carlos** sat on the chair.", we could say "**My friend** sat on the chair." The words **my friend** are a synonym (i.e., means the same thing) for **Carlos**.

2. Display an image. Ask students to identify the person, place or thing that is the topic of the picture. For example, for the following picture, students might identify **a girl**. Have students say a sentence using **girl** to describe what is happening in the picture.

The **girl** is eating some yogurt.

3. Model other ways to refer to the **girl**, such as **the little girl** or **the hungry girl**. Have them use the synonyms in another sentence telling about what is happening in the picture.

   **The hungry girl** looked happy eating the yogurt.

4. Remind students that there are other words that refer to people. In this case, that word is **she**. Illustrate how to use **she** in a sentence to tell more about the picture.

   **She** likes yogurt.

5. Repeat the sentences about the picture pointing out the connection between **girl**, **hungry girl** and **she**. These are three ways to refer to the same person.

6. Repeat the process with other images.


**Tips for Teaching**:

[1] This lesson can also be done using listening-level text. To do this, display the text (e.g., project the text or use a big book) that students are going to listen to. Have them follow along as you read the text to them. Identify a pronoun in the text and explicitly explain how the pronoun connects back to a namer (person, place or thing) in the text. Model rereading the sentence with the pronoun replacing it with the specific namer.

[2] Prior to working on this activity, some students may need instruction in pronoun recognition and pronoun function. For activities to develop this skill, see the **Meaning Links – Pronouns** activity in *Syntax: Knowledge to Practice*.

## Text Links (Stage 1)

**Objective**: To use vocabulary and syntactic clues that connect content and ideas across text.

**Target students**: K - 1

**Materials needed**: Listening level text[1, 2]

**How to do the activity**:

1.  Review with students that there are words that we use instead of our real people names or the name for the object. These words are called pronouns.[3] We use them instead of namers. For example, instead of saying "**Chinese people** celebrate the Chinese New Year.", we could say "**They** celebrate the Chinese New Year." The word **they** is a pronoun that refers to **Chinese people**. (Provide other examples as needed.) We can also refer to a namer using other words that mean the same thing. These are called synonyms. For example, instead of saying "**Chinese New Year** is an important celebration for Chinese people.", we could say "**This holiday** is an important celebration for Chinese people." The words **the holiday** are a synonym (i.e., means the same thing) for **Chinese New Year**. Writers use both pronouns and synonyms to make their writing more interesting.

2.  Display the text that students are going to listen to. Have them follow along as you read the text to them.

    > The Chinese New Year is an important holiday celebrated by Chinese people all around the world. During this time, Chinese families get together to spend time with one another. Together, they celebrate the past year. They also wish each other good luck for the New Year.

3.  After reading the text, teacher will identify a word or phrase that is important to understand the text (e.g., Chinese people). Highlight these words in the text.

    > The Chinese New Year is an important holiday celebrated by Chinese people all around the world. During this time, Chinese families get together to spend time with one another. Together, they celebrate the past year. They also wish each other good luck for the New Year.

4.  Continue reading and have students listen for other ways that the author refers to Chinese people (i.e., Chinese families, they). Highlight these words or phrases in the text.

    > The Chinese New Year is an important holiday celebrated by Chinese people all around the world. During this time, Chinese families get together to spend time with one another. Together, they celebrate the past year. They also wish each other good luck for the New Year.

5.  Repeat with another chain of references in the text. Point out how **this time** is another way of saying the **Chinese New Year**.

142

The Chinese New Year is an important holiday celebrated by Chinese people all around the world. During this time, Chinese families get together to spend time with one another. Together, they celebrate the past year. They also wish each other good luck for the New Year.

6.   Repeat the process with another paragraph from the text.

**Tips for Teaching**:

[1]This lesson is based on the informational selection *Chinese New Year* from www.ReadWorks.org

[2] This lesson can also be done using code-emphasis (decodable) text. Preselect a sequence of sentences containing a pronoun. Have students read the sentences. Point out the pronoun to the students and ask them to identify the namer (person, place or thing) that the pronoun refers to. Repeat with other preselected sentences. (See *Using big idea cue questions with code-emphasis text* pages 72 – 76 for a specific example of this task.)

[3]Prior to working on this activity, some students may need instruction in pronoun recognition and pronoun function. For activities to develop this skill, see the **Meaning Links – Pronouns** activity in *Syntax: Knowledge to Practice*.

**Text Links** (Stage 2)

**Objective**: To use vocabulary and syntactic clues that connect content and ideas across text.

**Target students**: 2 – 3

**Materials needed**: Authentic informational text selection[1, 2]

**How to do the activity**:

1.  Review with students that there are words that we use instead of real people names or the name for the object. These words are called pronouns[3]. We use them instead of namers. For example, instead of saying "**Plants** need sun and water to grow.", we could say "**They** need sun and water to grow." The word **they** is a pronoun that refers to **plants**. (Provide other examples as needed.) We can also refer to a namer using other words that mean the same thing. These are called synonyms. For example, instead of saying "**Plants** need sun and water to grow.", we could say "**Vegetation** needs sun and water to grown." The word vegetation is a synonym (i.e., means the same thing) for **plants**. Writers use both pronouns and synonyms to make their writing more interesting.

2.  Display the text that students are going to listen to. Have them follow along as you read the text to them.

    > Plants use these three puzzle pieces to make their own food in a process called photosynthesis. Using the energy from the sun, these living organisms convert water and carbon dioxide into sugar. This sugar feeds the plant's growth from a seedling into an adult. In the process, the vegetation releases oxygen into the air.

3.  After reading the text, ask students to identify the word or phrase that tells what the passage is about (i.e., plants). Highlight the first time this word or phrase appears.

    > Plants use these three puzzle pieces to make their own food in a process called photosynthesis. Using the energy from the sun, these living organisms convert water and carbon dioxide into sugar. This sugar feeds the plant's growth from a seedling into an adult. In the process, the vegetation releases oxygen into the air.

4.  Continue reading and have students listen for other ways the author refers to plants (i.e., their, plant's, these living organisms, vegetation). Highlight these additional examples in the text.

    > Plants use these three puzzle pieces to make their own food in a process called photosynthesis. Using the energy from the sun, these living organisms convert water and carbon dioxide into sugar. This sugar feeds the plant's growth from a seedling into an adult. In the process, the vegetation releases oxygen into the air.

5.  Reread the passage emphasizing the highlighted words.

6.  Repeat the process with another paragraph from the text.

**Tips for Teaching**:

[1]This lesson is based on an adaptation of *A Plant Puzzle!* from www.ReadWorks.org. The adaptation of the article involved replacing the word **plant** with synonyms (i.e., **these living organisms** and **vegetation**) to provide explicit practice in identifying synonyms as referential connectives.

[2]While previewing text selections, look for opportunities to adapt the text by replacing repeated words with pronouns and synonyms. Creating these kinds of "controlled text" conditions is important for students to learn to recognize referential connectives in text. (For more on text selection, see pages 61 – 62.)

[3]Prior to working on this activity, some students may need instruction in pronoun recognition and pronoun function. For activities to develop this skill, see the **Meaning Links – Pronouns** activity in *Syntax: Knowledge to Practice*.

# Inference

The following set of activities focuses on developing inferential thinking.

**Domain**: Comprehension

**Objective**: To use visual clues, verbal clues and background knowledge to develop inference-making skills.

**Background information for these activities**:

Reading comprehension requires students to understand what is stated explicitly as well as what is implied. This implicit understanding, referred to as inference, is a complex skill that develops over time with experience and practice. Inferencing requires higher order thinking skills that may be difficult for some students; however, these skills can be taught through explicit instruction.

Inferencing involves figuring something out or coming to a conclusion based on evidence. Evidence can be in the form of images or spoken or written words. To make an inference, information conveyed through the evidence activates prior background knowledge. For example, the image of a broken egg activates the viewer's knowledge that something happened to crack the shell, such as the egg fell on the floor or it was cracked on the side of a dish as part of making a cake. Additional information in the picture or story often clarifies what actually happened. The ability to inference (i.e., gap-filling) is required to understand what we read. Willingham reminds us that writers leave out the information they assume readers will know (Wexler, 2018). Inferencing helps the reader fill in missing information.

The ability to think about visual or verbal clues provides practice with inferential thinking. Students learn to activate what they know based on the clues to solve the puzzle. Using our egg example, seeing an image of a broken egg, students would activate their knowledge that eggs have a fragile shell that can break when dropped or struck. With beginning readers, riddle-like activities can simulate using what they know to figure out the answer to the question: *What is it?*. In Stage 0, a picture clue is the cue to describe what they actually see in order to guess what the clue represents. In Stage 1, verbal riddle-like clues about an image provide the evidence to predict what is pictured. And, in Stage 2, written riddle clues reveal more and more details to solve the puzzle. (See **What Is It?** activity page 147.)

The inference activities are designed to help students utilize what they know to fill in gaps or figure out an answer based on partial information. Through this series of activities, students gain insight about using what they know to figure out what is unstated. Using a similar progression from pictures to print, students can learn to use their background knowledge to interpret what they are seeing or reading. This type of practice requires a cognitive interaction with the visual or written information and practice "reading between the lines" by supplying background information. (See **Use What You Know** activity page 153.)

| Stage 0 | Stage 1 | Stage 2 |
|---|---|---|
| Using pictures<br>• Determine picture content from partial picture clues<br>• Use background knowledge to expand on picture content | Using pictures<br>• Determine picture content from riddle-like clues<br>• Use background knowledge to expand on decodable text content (i.e., what do we know; what do we need to fill in?) | Using pictures<br>• Determine answer from riddle-like clues<br>• Use background knowledge to expand on authentic text content (i.e., what do we know; what do we need to fill in?) |

146

## Inference: What Is It? (Stage 0)

**Objective**: To use visual clues and background knowledge to develop inference-making skills

**Target students**: PreK – K

**Materials needed**: Photos or pictures of objects, window template(s) for overlay

**How to do the activity**: [1]

1. Select a picture and cover it using the window template to reveal only a portion of the picture.[2] Make sure that the remainder of the picture is not visible to the students.

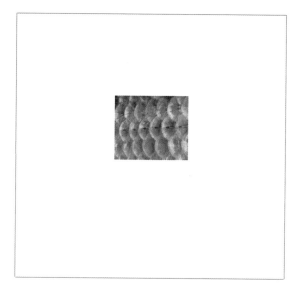

2. Discuss what the image in the window looks like. Encourage students to provide descriptive observations (e.g., orange, bumpy).

3. Have students guess what the picture might be (e.g., corn on the cob, bumps on a knit sweater). Ask students "What makes you say that?" "What do you notice?" to help students articulate what prompted their guesses.

4. Remove the window to reveal the image. Discuss the students' guesses compared to the actual image.

5. Repeat the process with other images.[3]

**Tips for Teaching:**

[1]This activity was inspired by Victoria Greene curriculum author of the Language Circle Enterprise, Inc.

[2]Window templates can be various sizes depending on the size of the picture and the amount of the picture that you want to expose as the clue. As an alternative to the template window, teachers can cover the picture with 3x5 self-stick notes and reveal parts of the picture by removing one self-stick note at a time. Discuss guesses after each portion of the picture is revealed and adjust thinking according to the new information.

[3]Jigsaw puzzles, presented a few pieces at a time, provide another technique to have students visualize and infer from partial visual information.

## Inference: What Is It?  (Stage 1)

**Objective**: To use verbal clues and background knowledge to solve a riddle to develop inference-making skills

**Target students**: K – 1

**Materials needed**: Photos or pictures, prepared riddle clues for pictured items[1]

**How to do the activity**:

1. Select a picture but do not reveal the image to the students. Tell students that you are going to give them clues to use to guess what the picture is.

2. Say the first clue: "I am an animal." Ask a few students what they think it is. Point out that it is hard to guess on the first clue because we don't have enough information.

3. Provide the next clue: "I can fly." Again, have students make guesses.

4. Continue with the other prepared clues having students guess after each one. "I do not have feathers." "I sleep upside down." When a student guesses the correct answer, reveal the picture.

5. Review the clues—in the order they were presented—to help students see how the clues added up to the correct identification of the pictured content.

6. Repeat with another picture.

**Tips for Teaching**:

[1]To generate word puzzles efficiently and instructively, use a combination of the target word's category and attributes (e.g., color, size, shape, texture, how move, how used, behavior). To write a riddle:
- Begin by identifying the category the word belongs in (e.g., animals, foods, feelings, places).
- Next, think of three to five clues.
- Finally, sequence the clues to elicit guesses from general to more specific.

For example, for the target word **bat**, the riddle might include the category animal and the following sequence of clues. (See Appendix page 205 for a riddle planning guide.)

|  | Literal clues |
|---|---|
| Category? | I am an **animal**. |
| How does target word move? | I can **fly**. |
| Texture? | I **do not** have **feathers**. |
| Behavior? | I **sleep upside down**. |
| What am I? | a bat |

This can be contrasted with **bat** as a kind of sports equipment.

| | Literal clues |
|---|---|
| Category? | I am a **kind of sports equipment**. |
| Texture? | I am **made of metal or wood**. |
| How move? | A player **swings** me. |
| How used? | I **hit a ball**. |
| | |
| What am I? | a baseball bat |

**Inference: What Is It?** (Stage 2)

**Objective**: To use verbal clues and background knowledge to solve a riddle to develop inference-making skills

**Target students**: 2 – 3

**Materials needed**: Prepared riddle clues written on individual sentence strips or as a PowerPoint with each clue animated,[1] cards with the answers to the riddles

**How to do the activity**:

1. Tell students that you are going to give them clues—one at a time—for them to guess what the answer is. Display the first clue in the prepared riddle.

> **I am something to eat.**

2. Ask several students to make guesses. Point out that it is hard to guess on the first clue because we don't have enough information.

3. Provide the next clue: "I am round." Again, have students make guesses.

> **I am round.**

4. Continue with the other prepared clues having students guess after each one. "I am as big as a baseball." "I am the color of a duck's bill." And "I make good juice." If a student guesses correctly, reveal the answer.

> **I am as big as a baseball.**

> **I am the color of a duck's bill.**

> **I make good juice.**

When a student guesses correctly, reveal the answer on the card.

> **I am an orange.**

5. Review the clues—in the order they were presented—to help students see how the clues added up to the correct identification of the pictured content.

6. Repeat with another riddle.

**Tips for Teaching:**

[1]To generate word puzzles efficiently and instructively, use a combination of the target word's category and attributes (e.g., color, size, shape, texture, how move, how used, behavior). When possible, provide a clue using figurative language (e.g., comparison, a simile). To develop a riddle:

- Begin by identifying the category the word belongs in (e.g., animals, foods, feelings, places).
- Next think of three to five clues. Write one or two in figurative language.
- Finally, sequence the clues to elicit guesses from general to more specific.

For example, for the target word **orange**, the riddle might include the category fruit and the following sequence of clues. (See Appendix page 205 for a riddle planning guide.)

| | Literal clues | Figurative clues |
|---|---|---|
| Category? | I am **something to eat**. | |
| Shape? | I am **round** | |
| Size? | | I am about as **big as a baseball**. |
| Color? | | I am the **color of a duck's bill**. |
| How used? | I make good juice. | |
| | | |
| What am I? | | an orange |

## Inference: Use What You Know (Stage 0)

**Objective**: To use visual clues and background knowledge to develop inference-making skills

**Target students**: PreK – K

**Materials needed**: Photos or pictures of objects[1]

**How to do the activity**:

1. Explain to students that sometimes they need to use what they know to understand what they see in a picture. To think about what happened, we do "gap-filling" – that is, we fill in the missing pieces to answer questions about what happened or what is happening.

2. Display a picture; for example, the picture of the two eggs—one whole and the other broken. Write two headings—What do I see? And What do I think is happening? —on a white board or chart paper. Ask students to describe what they see. Make notes of their observations under "What do I see?"

| What do I see? | What do I think happened? |
| --- | --- |
| a whole egg | |
| a broken egg shell | |
| the yolk (yellow part) of the egg | |

3. Tell students that even though we don't know what happened, we know something caused the egg to break. Ask students to suggest what might have happened to the egg. Record their ideas on the chart.

| What do I see? | What do I think happened? |
| --- | --- |
| a whole egg | one egg rolled off a table |
| a broken egg shell | someone dropped one of the eggs |
| the yolk (yellow part) of the egg | one egg fell out of the carton |

4. Explain that their ideas about what happened are called inferences. We use what we know to try to figure out what isn't shown in the picture.

5. Repeat the process with other images.

[1]Choose pictures that show that something happened to allow students to use their knowledge to explain what happened or what isn't pictured. For example, a picture of a popped balloon might elicit ideas about what caused the pop (e.g., something sharp punctured it, someone stepped on it) or a picture of a child dressed in warm clothes might elicit ideas about the kind of weather and activities the child would be doing to be dressed that way (e.g., going to play in the snow, live in a cold climate, and so on).

[2]A source of additional picture pairs are in *What's Different…What's the Same?*. See References and Resources in the Appendix for more information about this resource.

## Inference: Use What You Know (Stage 1)

**Objective**: To use clues in the text and background knowledge to develop inference-making skills

**Target students**: 1

**Materials needed**: Code-emphasis (decodable) text that the students can read with several short passages selected[1, 2]

**How to do the activity**:

1. Tell students that when they read, they need to use what they know to understand what the story is about.

2. Select a portion of the text and display it for the students to see.

> On the deck, the kids had bags.
> A mom had a black hat.
> Yum! Let's pick gum and a pop.

Ask students to identify what they know from the text. Write two headings—What is in the text? and What do I think is happening?[3] —on a white board or chart paper. Make notes of their observations under "What is in the text?"

| What is in the text? | What do I think is happening? |
| --- | --- |
| kids have bags | |
| mom is wearing a black hat | |
| the kids are picking candy—gum and a pop | |

3. Tell students that even though the text doesn't say it, we can figure out what is happening in the story. Ask students to suggest what the clues from the text might mean is happening. Record their ideas on the chart.

| What is in the text? | What do I think is happening? |
| --- | --- |
| kids have bags | the kids are collecting something |
| Mom is wearing a black hat | Mom is wearing a costume with a black hat |
| the kids are picking candy—gum and a pop | the kids are getting candy |
| | It's Halloween |

4. Ask students to guess what is happening (e.g., the kids are trick-or-treating for Halloween).

5. Explain that their ideas about what is happening in the text—even though it isn't written—are called inferences. We use what we know to try to figure out what isn't in the text.

6. Repeat with another portion of the story.

**Tips for Teaching**:

[1]The excerpt for this example is from *In the Den* from J. Lauren www.whole-phonics.com.

[2]The selected passages should be two to four sentences that require students to use their prior knowledge of schema or facts to understand the text. A couple of selected sets of sentences per story are sufficient to help students develop this skill.

[3]As students gain proficiency explaining "What is happening now?", expand the inferential questioning to include "What happened before?" and "What's happening next?"

## Inference: Use What You Know (Stage 2)

**Objective**: To use clues in the text and background knowledge to develop inference-making skills

**Target students**: 2 – 3

**Materials needed**: Authentic text that the students can read with several short paragraphs selected[1]

**How to do the activity**:

1.  Tell students that when they read, they need to use what they know to understand what the story is about.

2.  Select a portion of the text and display it for the students to see.

> Once upon a time there lived a poor widow who had an only son named Jack. She was very poor, for times had been hard, and Jack was too young to work. Almost all the furniture of the little cottage had been sold to buy bread, until, at last, there was nothing left worth selling.

Ask students to identify what they know from the text. Write two headings—What is in the text? and What do I think is happening?[2] —on a white board or chart paper. Make notes of their observations under "What is in the text?"

| What is in the text? | What do I think is happening? |
| --- | --- |
| woman was a widow | |
| woman was poor | |
| sold furniture to buy bread | |

3.  Tell students that even though the text doesn't say it directly, we can figure out what is happening in the story. Ask students to suggest what the clues from the text might mean is happening. Record their ideas on the chart.

| What is in the text? | What do I think is happening? |
| --- | --- |
| woman was a widow | woman's husband was not alive |
| woman was poor | trying to take care of Jack, her son |
| sold furniture to buy bread | needed money; no job |

4. Ask students to explain what is happening (e.g., the widow was selling everything because she didn't have a job and needed money).

5. Explain that their ideas about what is happening in the text—even though it isn't written—are called inferences. We use what we know to try to figure out what isn't in the text.

6. Repeat with another portion of the story.

**Tips for Teaching**:

[1]The excerpt for this activity is from *Jack and the Beanstalk* from www.ReadWorks.org

[2]As students gain proficiency explaining "What is happening now?", expand the inferential questioning to include "What happened before?" and "What do you think will happen next?"

## Reading/Writing Connection

The following sets of activities focus on the use of writing to develop reading comprehension.

**Domain**: Comprehension

**Objective**: To develop summary-writing skills using a sentence expansion approach and compose answers based on the knowledge of academic vocabulary for questions and sentence transformation.

**Background information for these activities**:

When readers draw upon information from what they read to write sentences, the writing simultaneously checks for understanding of the reading and facilitates remembering important content knowledge. Hochman and Wexler (2017) point out that "summarizing and sentence expansion demand similar skills: figuring out what's most important in a given body of information, what details support that main idea and how the details relate to one another." Explicit instruction in sentence expansion lays the foundation for composing oral or written summaries with content from both narrative and informational text. (See **Sentence Summaries** pages 161 – 172 and to develop these sentence-writing and expansion skills see *Syntax: Knowledge to Practice* for the activities **Sentence Building, Action: Tell Me More**, and **Namer: Tell Me More**.)

Answering questions about what we read depends on several abilities—understanding the text, remembering the content, and interpreting what the question is asking. This activity focuses on the last of these skills. The goal is for students to learn how to formulate responses—orally or in writing—that specifically provide the information signaled by the question or prompt words (See *The academic language of questions* pages 51 – 53). This question-answering activity (**What's the Answer**) is designed to teach students to use part of the question as the base of the answer. For example, the answer to the following question is formulated by replacing the question word "who" with the person that answers the question (i.e., "the girl").

<u>Who</u> is hungry?
<u>The girl</u> is hungry.

Through this sentence transformation process, students develop the ability to respond in complete sentences, which helps develop expressive language and complex sentence structure. It also improves oral language communication.

The process outlined in **What's the Answer?** applies to content from both narrative and informational text. Answering "W" questions based on narrative text reinforces the elements of a story. For example, **who** questions tap recall of characters in the story; **did what** questions draw on actions in the plot; **when** and **where** questions require understanding of the features of setting. In contrast, with informational text, these questions elicit factual information and contribute to students acquiring content knowledge. This reading – writing relationship based on content is crucial to developing background knowledge essential to comprehension (Hochman & Wexler, 2017).

The following table displays a progression of sentence writing activities across the three stages based on the type of text students typically read at each stage. The same activity can be utilized with text that students listen to.

| Stage 0 | Stage 1 | Stage 2 |
|---|---|---|
| With content from predictable text, orally compose sentences that tell?<br>  o  Who/what did it?<br>  o  What did he/she/it/they do?<br>  o  To whom/what<br>  o  When, where and how about the action<br>  o  How many, what kind, and which one about the namer | With code-emphasis text…<br>  o  Who/what did it?<br>  o  What did he/she/it/they do?<br>  o  To whom/what<br>  o  When, where and how about the action<br>  o  How many, what kind, and which one about the namer | With authentic text …<br>  o  Who/what did it?<br>  o  What did he/she/it/they do?<br>  o  To whom/what<br>  o  When, where and how about the action<br>  o  How many, what kind, and which one about the namer |

[1]For more information about teaching basic sentence structure see the activities **Sentence Building**, **Action: Tell Me More**, and **Namers: Tell Me More** in *Syntax: Knowledge to Practice*

The following table displays a progression for answering text-based questions utilizing stage-specific text.

| Stage 0 | Stage 1 | Stage 2 |
|---|---|---|
| With predictable text and listening-level text<br>• Use sentence transformation to answer in complete sentences (e.g., Who is the main character? Superman is the main character.) | With code-emphasis text and listening-level text<br>• Use sentence transformation to answer in complete sentences (e.g., Where did the cat sit? The cat sat on the mat.) | With authentic text and listening-level text<br>• Use sentence transformation to answer in complete sentences (e.g., How did the bean grow? The bean grew suddenly and gigantically.) |

## Sentence Summaries using Narrative Text (Stage 0)

**Objective**: To use content from narrative text to compose expanded sentences.

**Target students**: PreK - K

**Materials needed**: Predictable text selection in a displayable format (e.g., on chart paper, document camera display, or white board),[1] notecards or sentence strips, pocket chart

**How to do the activity**:

1. Display the text selection for all students to see. Read the selection to the students.

2. Remind students that they can use what they know about namers (nouns) and actions (verbs) to build sentences. Review that combining a namer and an action creates a complete thought.[2]

3. Provide students with a namer and action and object based on the content of the story.

| the girl | ate | yogurt |
|---|---|---|

4. Review that we can tell more about the action (i.e., **ate**) to make the sentence more interesting and accurate. To tell more about the action, we answer the following questions:

   - When?          *When* tells a specific time or period of time when the action happens.
   - Where?          *Where* tells a specific or general location where the action happens.
   - How?          *How* tells the way in which something is done.

5. Have students tell more about the action (i.e., ate) based on content from the text (e.g., **by herself** tells *how* she ate). Write the word or phrase on a card or sentence strip to add to the sentence.

| by herself |
|---|

6. Review that we can tell more about the namer (i.e., the girl) to make the sentence more descriptive. To tell more about the namer, we answer the following questions:

   - How many?          Tells a specific number or refers to an indefinite number.
   - What kind?          Describes observable (e.g., color, shape, size) or not observable (e.g., smart, kind, grouchy) attributes.
   - Which one?          Distinguishes from among named people, places or things (e.g., this, that, my).

7.  Have students tell more about the namer (i.e., the girl) based on content from the poem (e.g., **little** and **hungry** tell *what kind* of girl). Write the words or phrases on a card or sentence strips to add to the sentence.

8.  Arrange the cards to expand the simple sentence. Capitalize the first letter. Add a period at the end. Have students read the expanded sentence.

9.  Repeat the process with other simple sentences based on the selection.[3]

**Tips for Teaching**:

[1]This lesson is based on the poem *The Hungry Girl* from www.ReadWorks.org. For the text used for this activity, see Appendix page 207.

[2]This lesson is not designed to teach initial sentence writing skills. For an introduction to sentence writing development see the activities **Sentence Building, Action: Tell Me More**, and **Namers: Tell Me More** in *Syntax: Knowledge to Practice*.

[3]Ensuring that each student has a turn is especially important for English Learners who need abundant practice responding orally and in complete sentences.

## Sentence Summaries using Informational Text (Stage 0)

**Objective**: To use content from informational text to compose expanded sentences.

**Target students**: PreK - K

**Materials needed**: Listening-level text selection in a displayable format (e.g., on chart paper, document camera display, or white board),[1,2] notecards or sentence strips, pocket chart

### How to do the activity:

1. Display the text selection for all students to see. Read the selection to the students.

2. Remind students that they can use what they know about namers (nouns) and actions (verbs) to build sentences. Review that combining a namer and an action creates a complete thought.[3]

3. Provide students with a namer and action and object based on the content of the story.

| spices | flavor | food |
|--------|--------|------|

4. Review that we can tell more about the action (i.e., **flavor**) to make the sentence more interesting and accurate. To tell more about the action, we answer the following questions:
   - When?            *When* tells a specific time or period of time when the action happens.
   - Where?           *Where* tells a specific or general location where the action happens.
   - How?             *How* tells the way in which something is done.

5. Have students tell more about the action (i.e., **flavor**) based on content from the poem (e.g., **when we cook** tells *when* we flavor food). Write the word or phrase on a card or sentence strip to add to the sentence.

| when we cook |
|--------------|

6. Review that we can tell more about the namer (i.e., the spices) to make the sentence more descriptive. To tell more about the namer, we answer the following questions:
   - How many?        Tells a specific number or refers to an indefinite number.
   - What kind?        Describes observable (e.g., color, shape, size) or not observable (e.g., smart, kind, grouchy) attributes.
   - Which one?        Distinguishes from among named people, places or things (e.g., this, that, my).

7.  Have students tell more about the namer (i.e., spices) based on content from the text (e.g., **from seeds** and **from bark** and **from fruits** tell *which ones* about the spices). Write the words or phrases on a cards or sentence strips to add to the sentence.

8.  Arrange the cards to expand the simple sentence. Capitalize the first letter. Add a period at the end. Have students read the expanded sentence.

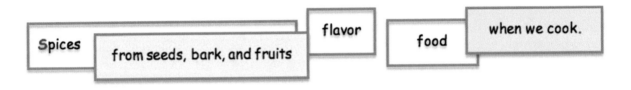

9.  Repeat the process with other simple sentences based on the text selection.[4]

**Tips for Teaching**:

[1]This lesson is based on the informational selection *So Many Spices* from www.ReadWorks.org. For the text used for this activity, see Appendix page 214.

[2]For more about the role of listening-level text, see *Concurrent paths—learning to decode and developing comprehension through listening* pages 59 – 60.

[3]This lesson is not designed to teach initial sentence writing skills. For an introduction to sentence writing development see the activities **Sentence Building, Action: Tell Me More**, and **Namers: Tell Me More** in *Syntax: Knowledge to Practice*.

[4]Ensuring that each student has a turn is especially important for English Learners who need abundant practice responding orally and in complete sentences.

[5]Completed **Knowledge Trees** can provide informational content to practice text-based sentence writing. (See pages 125 – 138 for the **Knowledge Tree** activity.)

## Sentence Summaries using Narrative Text (Stage 1)

**Objective**: To use content from narrative text to compose expanded sentences.

**Target students**: K -1

**Materials needed**: Decodable text selection in a displayable format (e.g., on chart paper, document camera display, or white board),[1] notecards or sentence strips, pocket chart

**How to do the activity**:

1. Display the text selection for all students to see. Read the selection to the students.

2. Remind students that they can use what they know about namers (nouns) and actions (verbs) to build sentences. Review that combining a namer and an action creates a complete thought.[2]

3. Provide students with a namer and action and object based on the content of the story.

| Mom | wore | hat |
|---|---|---|

4. Review that we can tell more about the action (i.e., **wore**) to make the sentence more interesting and accurate. To tell more about the action, we answer the following questions:

   - When?          *When* tells a specific time or period of time when the action happens.
   - Where?          *Where* tells a specific or general location where the action happens.
   - How?          *How* tells the way in which something is done.

5. Have students tell more about the action (i.e., ate) based on content from the poem (e.g., **for Halloween** tells *when* she wore the hat). Write the word or phrase on a card or sentence strip to add to the sentence.

| for Halloween |
|---|

6. Review that we can tell more about the namers (i.e., Mom, hat) to make the sentence more descriptive. To tell more about the namers, we answer the following questions:

   - How many?          Tells a specific number or refers to an indefinite number.
   - What kind?          Describes observable (e.g., color, shape, size) or not observable (e.g., smart, kind, grouchy) attributes.
   - Which one?          Distinguishes from among named people, places or things (e.g., this, that, my).

7. Have students tell more about the namer (i.e., hat) based on content from the poem (e.g., **black** tell *what kind of hat*). Write the words or phrases on a card or sentence strips to add to the sentence.

8. Arrange the cards to expand the simple sentence. Capitalize the first letter. Add a period at the end. Have students read the expanded sentence.

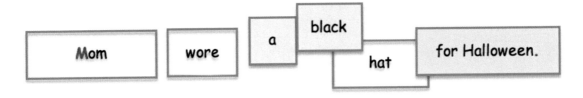

9. Repeat the process with other simple sentences based on the selection.[3]

**Tips for Teaching:**

[1]This lesson is based on the story *In the Den* from J. Lauren www.whole-phonics.com. For the text used for this activity, see Appendix page 208.

[2]This lesson is not designed to teach initial sentence writing skills. For an introduction to sentence writing development see the activities **Sentence Building**, **Action: Tell Me More**, and **Namers: Tell Me More** in *Syntax: Knowledge to Practice*.

[3]Ensuring that each student has a turn is especially important for English Learners who need abundant practice responding orally and in complete sentences.

## Sentence Summaries using Informational Text (Stage 1)

**Objective**: To use content from informational text to compose expanded sentences.

**Target students**: 1

**Materials needed**: Listening-level text selection in a displayable format (e.g., on chart paper, document camera display, or white board),[1,2] notecards or sentence strips, pocket chart

**How to do the activity**:

1. Display the text selection for all students to see. Read the selection to the students.

2. Remind students that they can use what they know about namers (nouns) and actions (verbs) to build sentences. Review that combining a namer and an action creates a complete thought.[3]

3. Provide students with a namer and action and object based on the content of the story.

| People | celebrate | New Year |
|---|---|---|

4. Review that we can tell more about the action (i.e., **celebrate**) to make the sentence more interesting and accurate. To tell more about the action, we answer the following questions:

   - When?          *When* tells a specific time or period of time when the action happens.
   - Where?         *Where* tells a specific or general location where the action happens.
   - How?           *How* tells the way in which something is done.

5. Have students tell more about the action (i.e., celebrate) based on content from the text (e.g., **by wearing red** tells *how* people celebrate). Write the word or phrase on a card or sentence strip to add to the sentence.

| by wearing red |
|---|

6. Review that we can tell more about the namers (i.e., people) to make the sentence more descriptive. To tell more about the namers, we answer the following questions:

   - How many?      Tells a specific number or refers to an indefinite number.
   - What kind?     Describes observable (e.g., color, shape, size) or not observable (e.g., smart, kind, grouchy) attributes.
   - Which one?     Distinguishes from among named people, places or things (e.g., this, that, my).

7.  Have students tell more about the namer (i.e., people) based on content from the text (e.g., **from China** tells *which people*). Write the words or phrases on a card or sentence strips to add to the sentence.

from China

8.  Arrange the cards to expand the simple sentence. Capitalize the first letter. Add a period at the end. Have students read the expanded sentence.

People    from China    celebrate    New Year    by wearing red.

9.  Repeat the process with other simple sentences based on the selection.[4]

**Tips for Teaching**:

[1]This lesson is based on the informational selection *Chinese New Year* from www.ReadWorks.org. For the text used for this activity, see Appendix page 215.

[2]For more about the role of listening-level text, see *Concurrent paths learning to decode and developing comprehension through listening* pages 59 – 60.

[3]This lesson is not designed to teach initial sentence writing skills. For an introduction to sentence writing development see the activities **Sentence Building, Action: Tell Me More**, and **Namers: Tell Me More** in *Syntax: Knowledge to Practice*.

[4]Ensuring that each student has a turn is especially important for English Learners who need abundant practice responding orally and in complete sentences.

[5]Completed **Knowledge Trees** can provide informational content to practice text-based sentence writing. (See pages 125 – 138 for the **Knowledge Tree** activity.)

## Sentence Summaries using Narrative Text (Stage 2)

**Objective**: To use content from narrative text to compose expanded sentences.

**Target students**: 2 – 3

**Materials needed**: Authentic text selection in a displayable format (e.g., on chart paper, document camera display, or white board),[1] notecards or sentence strips, pocket chart

**How to do the activity**:

1.  Display the text selection for all students to see. Read the selection to the students.

2.  Remind students that they can use what they know about namers (nouns) and actions (verbs) to build sentences. Review that combining a namer and an action creates a complete thought.[2]

3.  Provide students with a namer and action and when possible, an object based on the content of the story.

| beanstalk | grew |
|---|---|

4.  Review that we can tell more about the action (i.e., **grew**) to make the sentence more interesting and accurate. To tell more about the action, we answer the following questions:

    - When?          *When* tells a specific time or period of time when the action happens.
    - Where?         *Where* tells a specific or general location where the action happens.
    - How?           *How* tells the way in which something is done.

5.  Have students tell more about the action (i.e., grew) based on content from the story (e.g., **into the sky** tells *where* the beanstalk grew). Write the word or phrase on a card or sentence strip to add to the sentence.

| into the sky |
|---|

6.  Review that we can tell more about the namer (i.e., the beanstalk) to make the sentence more descriptive. To tell more about the namer, we answer the following questions:

    - How many?      Tells a specific number or refers to an indefinite number.
    - What kind?     Describes observable (e.g., color, shape, size) or not observable (e.g., smart, kind, grouchy) attributes.
    - Which one?     Distinguishes from among named people, places or things (e.g., this, that, my).

7. Have students tell more about the namer (i.e., beanstalk) based on content from the story (e.g., **great** tells what kind and **outside Jack's window** tells *which ones*). Write the words or phrases on a card or sentence strips to add to the sentence.

8. Arrange the cards to expand the simple sentence.  Capitalize the first letter. Add a period at the end. Have students read the expanded sentence.

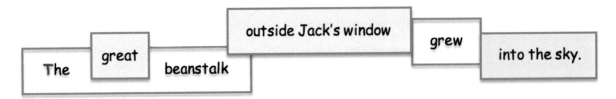

9. Repeat the process with other simple sentences based on the selection.[3]

**Tips for Teaching**:

[1]This lesson is based on the story *Jack and the Beanstalk* from www.ReadWorks.org. For the text used for this activity, see Appendix page 209.

[2]This lesson is not designed to teach initial sentence writing skills. For an introduction to sentence writing development see the activities **Sentence Building, Action: Tell Me More,** and **Namers: Tell Me More** in *Syntax: Knowledge to Practice.*

[3]Ensuring that each student has a turn is especially important for English Learners who need abundant practice responding orally and in complete sentences.

## Sentence Summaries using Informational Text (Stage 2)

**Objective**: To use content from informational text to compose expanded sentences.

**Target students**: 2 – 3

**Materials needed**: Authentic text selection in a displayable format (e.g., on chart paper, document camera display, or white board),[1, 2] notecards or sentence strips, pocket chart

**How to do the activity**:

1.  Display the text selection for all students to see. Read the selection to the students.

2.  Remind students that they can use what they know about namers (nouns) and actions (verbs) to build sentences. Review that combining a namer and an action creates a complete thought.[3]

3.  Provide students with a namer and action and object based on the content of the story.

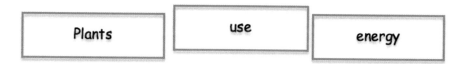

4.  Review that we can tell more about the action (i.e., **use**) to make the sentence more interesting and accurate. To tell more about the action, we answer the following questions:

    *   When?          *When* tells a specific time or period of time when the action happens.
    *   Where?         *Where* tells a specific or general location where the action happens.
    *   How?           *How* tells the way in which something is done.

5.  Have students tell more about the action (i.e., **use**) based on content from the text (e.g., **when they grow** tells *when* the plants use energy). Write the word or phrase on a card or sentence strip to add to the sentence.

> **when they grow**

6.  Review that we can tell more about the namer (i.e., plants) to make the sentence more descriptive. To tell more about the namer, we answer the following questions:

    *   How many?      Tells a specific number or refers to an indefinite number.
    *   What kind?      Describes observable (e.g., color, shape, size) or not observable (e.g., smart, kind, grouchy) attributes.
    *   Which one?      Distinguishes from among named people, places or things (e.g., this, that, my).

7.  Have students tell more about the namer (i.e., energy) based on content from the selection (e.g., **from sunlight** tells *which ones*). Write the words or phrases on a card or sentence strips to add to the sentence.

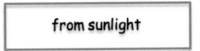

8.  Arrange the cards to expand the simple sentence. Capitalize the first letter. Add a period at the end. Have students read the expanded sentence.

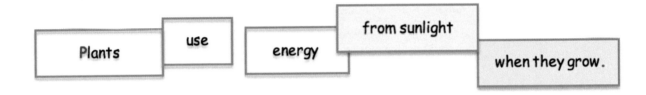

9.  Repeat the process with other simple sentences based on the selection.[4]


**Tips for Teaching**:

[1]This lesson is based on *A Plant Puzzle!* from www.ReadWorks.org. For the text used for this activity, see Appendix page 215.

[2]Depending on the difficulty level of the text selection, students can either read the text themselves or listen to the teacher read it. With informational text, there is a dual goal—exposure to more content-rich text and writing based on that content. To achieve these goals, use of a blend of listening-level and text students can read themselves is essential. For more about the role of listening-level text, see *Concurrent paths—learning to decode and developing comprehension through listening* pages 59 – 60.

[3]This lesson is not designed to teach initial sentence writing skills. For an introduction to sentence writing development see the activities **Sentence Building, Action: Tell Me More**, and **Namers: Tell Me More** in *Syntax: Knowledge to Practice*.

[4]Ensuring that each student has a turn is especially important for English Learners who need abundant practice responding orally and in complete sentences.

[5]Completed **Knowledge Trees** can provide informational content to practice text-based sentence writing. (See pages 125 – 138 for the **Knowledge Trees** activity.)

## Answering Questions: What's the Answer? using Narrative Text (Stage 0)

**Objective**: To develop answers (oral or written) based on knowledge of academic vocabulary that signal questions and prompts.

**Target students**: PreK – K

**Materials needed**: Predictable text selection in a displayable format (e.g., on chart paper, document camera display, or white board)[1, 2], prepared questions for the text on sentence strips, pocket chart

**How to do the activity**:

1. Display the text selection for the students to follow along as they listen/read it with the teacher. After reading the selection to the students, display a question using one of the "wh" question words (e.g., **who**).[3]

> Who is hungry?

2. Underline the word **who**. Tell students that the answer to this question that begins with the word **who** needs to name a person.

> <u>Who</u> is hungry?

3. Ask students to use the information from the text that tells **who** is hungry. Write their answer on a strip of paper or a card.

> the little girl

4. Hold the card over the word **who** in the question to show how **the girl** replaces the question word with information.

> the little girl is hungry?

5.  Write the sentence with correct capitalization and punctuation. Explain that the end punctuation must change from a question mark to a period because the sentence is now telling not asking something.

6.  Repeat the process with other questions beginning with **who** (e.g., **Who** ate the muffin? **Who** ate the yogurt? **Who** did the little girl talk to?).[4]

**Tips for Teaching**:

[1]This lesson is based on the poem *The Hungry Girl* from www.ReadWorks.org. For the text used for this activity, see Appendix page 209.

[2]Students can practice **What's the Answer?** based on text that they listen to as well as what they can read themselves. For more information about selecting listening-level text see *Concurrent paths—learning to decode and developing comprehension through listening* pages 59 – 60.

[3]It is important to focus on one question word at a time (e.g., **who**) until students understand that the response must name a person (See table on page 52 for examples). When students are consistently providing the correct information for **who** questions, introduce another question word. Practice the new question word (e.g., **did what**) until students understand the kind of information required in the answer. Then practice with both **who** and **did what** questions to ensure that students provide the right kind of information before introducing another one.

[4]This activity can be done orally. The goal is for students to answer in complete sentences.

## Answering Questions: What's the Answer using Informational Text? (Stage 0)

**Objective**: To develop answers (oral or written) based on knowledge of academic vocabulary that signal questions and prompts.

**Target students**: PreK – K

**Materials needed**: Predictable text selection in a displayable format (e.g., on chart paper, document camera display, or white board)[1, 2], prepared questions for the text on sentence strips, pocket chart

**How to do the activity**:

1.  Display the text selection for the students to follow along as they listen/read it with the teacher. After reading the selection to the students, display a question using one of the "wh" question words (e.g., **which**).[3]

> ### Which foods help the heart and give us energy?

2.  Underline the word **which**. Tell students that **which** is a signal that the question is asking about the namer that comes next (i.e., foods). Underline the namer following **which**. Tell students that the answer to this question that begins with the word **which** followed by a namer needs to provide information about that namer (e.g., which one, what kind, or how many).

> ### <u>Which foods</u> help the heart and give us energy?

3.  Ask students to use the information from the text that tells **which foods** help the heart and give us energy. Write their answer on a strip of paper or a card.

> ### whole grains

4.  Hold the card over the word **which** in the question to show how **whole grains** replaces the question word with information.

> ### whole grains help the heart and give us energy?

5.  Write the sentence with correct capitalization and punctuation. Explain that the end punctuation must change from a question mark to a period because the sentence is now telling not asking something.

6.  Repeat the process with other questions beginning with **which** (e.g., **What** are some whole grain snacks?).[4]

**Tips for Teaching**:

[1]This lesson excerpt is from *Eat Right, Feel Great!* From www.ReadWorks.org. For the text used for this activity, see Appendix page 212.

[2]Students can practice **What's the Answer?** based on text that they listen to as well as what they can read themselves. For more information about selecting listening-level text, see *Concurrent paths—learning to decode and developing comprehension through listening* pages 59 – 60.

[3]It is important to focus on one question word at a time (e.g., **who**) until students understand that the response must name a person (See table on page 52 for examples). When students are consistently providing the correct information for **who** questions, introduce another question word. Practice the new question word (e.g., **did what**) until students understand the kind of information required in the answer. Then practice with both **who** and **did what** questions to ensure that students provide the right kind of information before introducing another one.

[4]This activity can be done orally. The goal is for students to answer in complete sentences.

## Answering Questions: What's the Answer? using Narrative Text (Stage 1)

**Objective**: To develop answers (oral or written) based on knowledge of academic vocabulary that signal questions and prompts.

**Target students**: K-1

**Materials needed**: Decodable text[1, 2], prepared questions for the text, pocket chart

**How to do the activity**:

1.  Display the text selection for the students to read. After reading the selection, display a question using one of the "wh" question words (e.g., **who**).[3]

**Who was on the deck?**

2.  Underline the word **who**. Tell students that the answer to this question that begins with the word **who** needs to name a person.

**<u>Who</u> was on the deck?**

3.  Ask students to use the information from the story that tells **who** was on the deck. Write their answer on a strip of paper or a card.

**the kids**

4.  Hold the card over the word **who** in the question to show how **the kids** replaces the question word with information from the story.

5.  Write the sentence with correct capitalization and punctuation. Adjust the verb from **was** to **were** to agree with the plural subject **kids**. Explain that the end punctuation must change from a question mark to a period because the sentence is now telling not asking something.

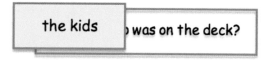

6. Repeat the process with other questions beginning with **who** (e.g., **Who** was wearing a black hat? **Who** had a web on her neck? **Who** had fun on the deck?).[4]

**Tips for Teaching**:

[1]This lesson is based on the story *In the Den* from J. Lauren www.whole-phonics.com. For the text used for this activity, see Appendix page 208.

[2]Students can practice **What's the Answer?** based on text that they listen to as well as what they can read themselves. For more information about selecting listening-level text, see *Concurrent paths—learning to decode and developing comprehension through listening* pages 59 – 60.

[3]It is important to focus on one question word at a time (e.g., **who**) until students understand that the response must name a person (See table on page 52 for examples). When students are consistently providing the correct information for **who** questions, introduce another question word. Practice the new question word (e.g., **did what**) until students understand the kind of information required in the answer. Then practice with both **who** and **did what** questions to ensure that students provide the right kind of information before introducing another one.

[4]This activity can be done orally. The goal is for students to answer in complete sentences.

## Answering Questions: What's the Answer? using Informational Text (Stage 1)

**Objective**: To develop answers (oral or written) based on knowledge of academic vocabulary that signal questions and prompts.

**Target students**: K-1

**Materials needed**: Decodable text[1, 2], prepared questions for the text, pocket chart

**How to do the activity**:

1. Display the text selection for the students to read. After reading the selection, display a question using one of the "wh" question words (e.g., **which**).[3]

> ### Which celebration takes place in Peru in June?

2. Underline the word **which**. Tell students that **which** is a signal that the question is asking about the namer that comes next (i.e., celebration). Underline the namer following **which**. Tell students that the answer to this question that begins with the word **which** followed by a namer needs to provide information about that namer (e.g., which one, what kind, or how many).

> ### <u>Which celebration</u> takes place in Peru in June?

3. Ask students to use the information from the text that tells **which celebration** happens in Peru in June. Write their answer on a strip of paper or a card.

> ### the festival of the Sun

4. Hold the card over the word **which** in the question to show how **the festival of the Sun** replaces the question word with information from the text.

> ### the festival of the Sun takes place in Peru in June?

5. Write the sentence with correct capitalization and punctuation. Explain that the end punctuation must change from a question mark to a period because the sentence is now telling not asking something.

| The festival of the Sun | celebration takes place in Peru in June. |

6. Repeat the process with other questions beginning with **which** or another question word (e.g., **Why** do people celebrate the festival of the Sun? **When** does the festival of the Sun happen?).[4]

**Tips for Teaching**:

[1]This lesson is based on an excerpt is from *Celebrations Around the World* From www.ReadWorks.org. For the text used for this activity, see Appendix page 212.

[2]Students can practice **What's the Answer?** based on text that they listen to as well as what they can read themselves. For more information about selecting listening-level text, see *Concurrent paths—learning to decode and developing comprehension through listening* pages 59 - 60.

[3]It is important to focus on one question word at a time (e.g., **who**) until students understand that the response must name a person (See table on page 52 for examples). When students are consistently providing the correct information for **who** questions, introduce another question word. Practice the new question word (e.g., **did what**) until students understand the kind of information required in the answer. Then practice with both **who** and **did what** questions to ensure that students provide the right kind of information before introducing another one.

[4]This activity can be done orally. The goal is for students to answer in complete sentences.

**Answering Questions: What's the Answer? using Narrative Text (Stage 2)**

**Objective**: To develop answers (oral or written) based on knowledge of academic vocabulary that signal questions and prompts.

**Target students**: 2 – 3

**Materials needed**: Authentic text selection[1, 2], prepared questions[3], pocket chart

**How to do the activity**:

1. Display the text selection for the students to read. After reading the selection, display a question using one of the "wh" question words (e.g., **who**).[3]

> # Who made a bargain for the cow?

2. Underline the word **who**. Tell students that the answer to this question that begins with the word **who** needs to name a person.

> # <u>Who</u> made a bargain for the cow?

3. Ask students to use the information from the story that tells **who** is made the bargain for the cow. Write their answer on a strip of paper or a card.

> # Jack

4. Hold the card over the word **who** in the question to show how **Jack** replaces the question word with information.

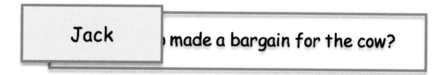

5. Write the sentence with correct capitalization and punctuation. Explain that the end punctuation must change from a question mark to a period because the sentence is now telling not asking something.

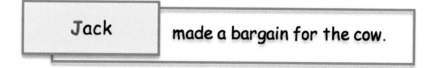

6. Repeat the process with other questions beginning with **who** (e.g., **Who** made the bargain with Jack? **Who** was disappointed with the bargain? **Who** was the gallant knight?).[4]


**Tips for Teaching**:

[1] This lesson is based on the story *Jack and the Beanstalk* from www.ReadWorks.org. For the text used for this activity, see Appendix page 209.

[2] Students can practice **What's the Answer?** based on text that they listen to as well as what they can read themselves. For more information about selecting listening-level text, see *Concurrent paths—learning to decode and developing comprehension through listening* pages 59 – 60.

[3] It is important to focus on one question word at a time (e.g., **who**) until students understand that the response must name a person (See table on page 52 for examples). When students are consistently providing the correct information for **who** questions, introduce another question word. Practice the new question word (e.g., **did what**) until students understand the kind of information required in the answer. Then practice with both **who** and **did what** questions to ensure that students provide the right kind of information before introducing another one.

[4] This activity can be done orally. The goal is for students to answer in complete sentences.

## Answering Questions: What's the Answer? using Informational Text (Stage 2)

**Objective**: To develop answers (oral or written) based on knowledge of academic vocabulary that signal questions and prompts.

**Target students**: 2 – 3

**Materials needed**: Authentic text selection[1,2], prepared questions, pocket chart

**How to do the activity**:

1.  Display the text selection for the students to read. After reading the selection, display a question using one of the "wh" question words (e.g., **which**).[3]

> ## Which three puzzle pieces are needed for a plant to grow?

2.  Underline the word **which**. Tell students that **which** is a signal that the question is asking about the namer that comes next (i.e., puzzle pieces). Underline the namer following **which**. Tell students that the answer to this question that begins with the word **which** followed by a namer needs to provide information about that namer (e.g., which one, what kind, or how many.)

> ## <u>Which</u> three <u>puzzle pieces</u> are needed for a plant to grow?

3.  Ask students to use the information from the text that tells **which puzzle pieces** are needed for a plant to grow. Write their answer on a strip of paper or a card.

> ## water, carbon dioxide and light

4.  Hold the card over the word **which** in the question to show how **water, carbon dioxide and light** replace the question word with information from the text.

> ## water, carbon dioxide and light three puzzle pieces are needed for a plant to grow?

5.  Write the sentence with correct capitalization and punctuation. Explain that the end punctuation must change from a question mark to a period because the sentence is now telling not asking something. Also, change the position of the word **are** in the sentence.

| Water, carbon dioxide and light | are three puzzle pieces needed for a plant to grow. |

6. Repeat the process with other questions beginning with **which** or other questions words (e.g., **How** do plants take in sunlight and carbon dioxide? **Why** are roots important to plants?).[4]

**Tips for Teaching**:

[1]This lesson is based on an excerpt from *A Plant Puzzle* from www.ReadWorks.org. For the text used for this activity, see Appendix page 217.

[3]Students can practice **What's the Answer?** based on text that they listen to as well as what they can read themselves. For more information about selecting listening-level text, see *Concurrent paths—learning to decode and developing comprehension through listening* pages 59 – 60.

[2]It is important to focus on one question word at a time (e.g., **who**) until students understand that the response must name a person (See table on page 52 for examples). When students are consistently providing the correct information for **who** questions, introduce another question word. Practice the new question word (e.g., **did what**) until students understand the kind of information required in the answer. Then practice with both **who** and **did what** questions to ensure that students provide the right kind of information before introducing another one.

[4]This activity can be done orally. The goal is for students to answer in complete sentences.

# Appendix

Contents:

- Retelling Rubrics for Progress Monitoring
- Practice Using the Retelling Rubrics
- Possible Answers for the Retelling Rubric Practice Items
- Possible Analysis for Try It Cue Questions for Text Analysis
- Story Map graphic organizers
- Knowledge Tree graphic organizer
- Riddle Planning Guide
- Text Selections for Reference and Practice
- References and Resources

**Retelling Rubrics for Progress Monitoring**

How to administer retelling rubrics[1]:

1. Select the rubric for the type of text the student will listen to or read.

2. Have students listen to or read the text selection.

3. Ask students to retell the text that they listened to or read. Use the rubric as a guide to make notes and/or record the student's retelling. Use the rubric criteria to rate the student's retelling.

4. Record the ratings in the log. Be sure to indicate whether the retelling is based on listening (e.g., "L") or reading (e.g., "R").

5. Use the log to keep a history of multiple retellings to monitor progress.

[1]See *The Role of Retelling Rubrics in Monitoring Student Progress in Comprehending Text* on pages 99 – 106 for more information about and examples using the rubrics.

# Retelling Rubric

| Objective | Beginning 1 | Developing 2 | Mastery 3 | Exemplary 4 |
|---|---|---|---|---|
| *Uses complete sentences in retelling the passage* | Uses incomplete sentences—many are not comprehensible | Uses complete and incomplete sentences | Uses complete sentences with simple structure | Uses complete sentences with varied structures |
| *Captures the salient idea of each event* | Does not recall all salient ideas or inaccurately expresses two or more ideas | Expresses one salient idea incompletely or inaccurately | Accurately captures the salient idea of each event but is verbose or not specific enough | Accurately and succinctly captures the salient idea of each event |
| *Sequences events cohesively* | Does not include all events or does not state all events in correct order | States events in order but without any transitions | Sequences events using transition words (e.g., *first, then, next, finally*) | Sequences events using words such as, *then, next, therefore, that's why, so, if, because* |
| *Incorporates vocabulary from the passage* | Does not incorporate any vocabulary words from the passage | Incorporates vocabulary words exactly as used in the passage | Uses appropriate synonyms for words from the passage | Uses vocabulary words from the passage in novel ways |
| *Retells the passage with prosody* | Does not complete the retelling and may say "I can't remember" or "I forget" | Restates, pauses, or self-corrects while retelling the passage and may overuse "um" | Retells the passage haltingly but persistently | Retells the passage with ease, confidence, and expression |

Carreker (2011). Used by permission of Neuhaus Education Center, Bellaire, TX.

| Date | Text | Uses complete sentences | Captures each event | Sequences events cohesively | Incorporates vocabulary from text | Retells with prosody |
|---|---|---|---|---|---|---|
| | | | | | | |
| | | | | | | |
| | | | | | | |

## Retelling Rubric
## Narrative Text

Circle the description in each row that best captures student's retelling.

|  | Beginning<br>1 | Developing<br>2 | Proficient<br>3 |
|---|---|---|---|
| Setting and Characters | One main character with a reference to a general place or time and a problem that elicits a character's response, but one that is not directly related to the event | One main character with a specific name and reference(s) to specific places or times and at least one stated event or problem that elicits a character's response | More than one main character with specific names, references to specific places and times, and two or more distinct stated events or problems that elicit the characters' responses |
| Initiating Event and Actions | One statement about the character's emotions or feelings but the responses are not related to an event or problem and one statement about how the character might solve the problem; however, the character's actions are not related to the problem itself | One or more statements about the character's emotions or feelings related to an event or problem and two statements about how the character might solve the problem that includes attempts by the character to solve the problem | One or more statements about the character's emotions or feelings related to an event or problem and three or more statements about how the character might solve the problem that includes attempts by the character to solve the problem |
| Conclusion and Resolution | One statement about what happened at the end of the story | One statement about what happened at the end of the story and how the character(s) felt as a result of the consequence | One statement about what happened at the end of the story including any additional problems/complications that occurred and how the character(s) felt as a result of the consequence |

Based on rubric referenced in Petersen, D.B., Gillam, S.L., & Gillam, R.B. (2008). Emerging Procedures in Narrative Assessment: The Index of Narrative Complexity. *Topics in Language Disorders, 28*, 115-130.

| Date | Text | Setting and Characters | Initiating Event and Actions | Conclusion and Resolution | Total points |
|---|---|---|---|---|---|
|  |  |  |  |  |  |
|  |  |  |  |  |  |
|  |  |  |  |  |  |

# Retelling Rubric for Knowledge Trees
## Informational Text

Circle the description in each row that best captures student's retelling.

|  | Beginning 1 | Developing 2 | Proficient 3 |
|---|---|---|---|
| Topic | No topic stated | General statement of topic | Precise label of topic |
| Major subtopic | No subtopics stated | Some subtopics stated | All subtopics stated |
| Supporting details | No supporting details included | Some supporting details included | All or most supporting details included |
| Language Usage | Little or no organization of information from the text selection | Information conveyed using some cohesive ties to show content relationship | Clear use of specific vocabulary and cohesive ties to convey the content information |

| Date | Text | Topic | Major subtopics | Supporting Details | Language Usage | Total points |
|---|---|---|---|---|---|---|
|  |  |  |  |  |  |  |
|  |  |  |  |  |  |  |
|  |  |  |  |  |  |  |

## Practice Using the Retelling Rubrics

- Read the sample student retelling in italics.
- Use the rubric to rate it.
- Transfer the rating to the log.
- Consider what the instructional implications are for the student based on the rating.

## Sample student retelling set #1

*1/10/2020 – A Sick Rock?*

*"Some kids tripped over a rock, but it wasn't a rock. It was a duck. The kids wanted to help the sick duck. They took it to the vet. The vet gave the duck a bath. Then it went to the zoo."*

|  | Beginning 1 | Developing 2 | Proficient 3 |
|---|---|---|---|
| Setting and Characters | One main character with a reference to a general place or time and a problem that elicits a character's response, but one that is not directly related to the event | One main character with a specific name and reference(s) to specific places or times and at least one stated event or problem that elicits a character's response | More than one main character with specific names, references to specific places and times, and two or more distinct stated events or problems that elicit the characters' responses |
| Initiating Event and Actions | One statement about the character's emotions or feelings but the responses are not related to an event or problem and one statement about how the character might solve the problem; however, the character's actions are not related to the problem itself | One or more statements about the character's emotions or feelings related to an event or problem and two statements about how the character might solve the problem that includes attempts by the character to solve the problem | One or more statements about the character's emotions or feelings related to an event or problem and three or more statements about how the character might solve the problem that includes attempts by the character to solve the problem |
| Conclusion and Resolution | One statement about what happened at the end of the story | One statement about what happened at the end of the story and how the character(s) felt as a result of the consequence | One statement about what happened at the end of the story including any additional problems/complications that occurred and how the character(s) felt as a result of the consequence |

*2/10/2020 – In the Den*

*"Liz, Ann, and Tim have on costumes for Halloween. They went into a den and got scared. They couldn't get out, so they yelled for help. A black cat used magic to open the door, so the kids got out. They went back to the deck and got candy."*

|  | | Beginning<br>1 | Developing<br>2 | Proficient<br>3 |
|---|---|---|---|---|
| Setting and Characters | | One main character with a reference to a general place or time and a problem that elicits a character's response, but one that is not directly related to the event | One main character with a specific name and reference(s) to specific places or times and at least one stated event or problem that elicits a character's response | More than one main character with specific names, references to specific places and times, and two or more distinct stated events or problems that elicit the characters' responses |
| Initiating Event and Actions | | One statement about the character's emotions or feelings but the responses are not related to an event or problem and one statement about how the character might solve the problem; however, the character's actions are not related to the problem itself | One or more statements about the character's emotions or feelings related to an event or problem and two statements about how the character might solve the problem that includes attempts by the character to solve the problem | One or more statements about the character's emotions or feelings related to an event or problem and three or more statements about how the character might solve the problem that includes attempts by the character to solve the problem |
| Conclusion and Resolution | | One statement about what happened at the end of the story | One statement about what happened at the end of the story and how the character(s) felt as a result of the consequence | One statement about what happened at the end of the story including any additional problems/complications that occurred and how the character(s) felt as a result of the consequence |

| Date | Text | Setting and Characters | Initiating Event and Actions | Conclusion and Resolution | Total points |
|---|---|---|---|---|---|
|  |  |  |  |  |  |
|  |  |  |  |  |  |
|  |  |  |  |  |  |

## Sample student retelling set #2

1/10/2020 – Clouds and Rain – Student A

*"Clouds are in the sky. They are white. They are fluffy."*

|  | Beginning 1 | Developing 2 | Proficient 3 |
|---|---|---|---|
| Topic | No topic stated | General statement of topic | Precise label of topic |
| Major subtopic | No subtopics stated | Some subtopics stated | All subtopics stated |
| Supporting details | No supporting details included | Some supporting details included | All or most supporting details included |
| Language Usage | Little or no organization of information from the text selection | Information conveyed using some cohesive ties to show content relationship | Clear use of specific vocabulary and cohesive ties to convey the content information |

1/10/2020 – Clouds and Rain – Student B

*"Clouds are made of water. They can be white and fluffy. Some clouds are gray. They make it rain."*

|  | Beginning 1 | Developing 2 | Proficient 3 |
|---|---|---|---|
| Topic | No topic stated | General statement of topic | Precise label of topic |
| Major subtopic | No subtopics stated | Some subtopics stated | All subtopics stated |
| Supporting details | No supporting details included | Some supporting details included | All or most supporting details included |

| | Beginning 1 | Developing 2 | Proficient 3 |
|---|---|---|---|
| Language Usage | Little or no organization of information from the text selection | Information conveyed using some cohesive ties to show content relationship | Clear use of specific vocabulary and cohesive ties to convey the content information |

## Student A

| Date | Text | Topic | Major subtopics | Supporting Details | Language Usage | Total points |
|---|---|---|---|---|---|---|
| | | | | | | |
| | | | | | | |
| | | | | | | |

## Student B

| Date | Text | Topic | Major subtopics | Supporting Details | Language Usage | Total points |
|---|---|---|---|---|---|---|
| | | | | | | |
| | | | | | | |
| | | | | | | |

# Possible Answers for Retelling Rubric Practice Items

## Sample student retelling set #1

1/10/2020 – *A Sick Rock?*

*"Some kids tripped over a rock, but it wasn't a rock. It was a duck. The kids wanted to help the sick duck. They took it to the vet. The vet gave the duck a bath. Then it went to the zoo."*

| | Beginning 1 | Developing 2 | Proficient 3 |
|---|---|---|---|
| **Setting and Characters** | One main character with a reference to a general place or time and a problem that elicits a character's response, but one that is not directly related to the event | One main character with a specific name and reference(s) to specific places or times and at least one stated event or problem that elicits a character's response | More than one main character with specific names, references to specific places and times, and two or more distinct stated events or problems that elicit the characters' responses |
| **Initiating Event and Actions** | One statement about the character's emotions or feelings but the responses are not related to an event or problem and one statement about how the character might solve the problem; however, the character's actions are not related to the problem itself | One or more statements about the character's emotions or feelings related to an event or problem and two statements about how the character might solve the problem that includes attempts by the character to solve the problem | One or more statements about the character's emotions or feelings related to an event or problem and three or more statements about how the character might solve the problem that includes attempts by the character to solve the problem |
| **Conclusion and Resolution** | One statement about what happened at the end of the story | One statement about what happened at the end of the story and how the character(s) felt as a result of the consequence | One statement about what happened at the end of the story including any additional problems/complications that occurred and how the character(s) felt as a result of the consequence |

194

2/10/2020 – *In the Den*

*"Liz, Ann, and Tim have on costumes for Halloween. They went into a den and got scared. They couldn't get out, so they yelled for help. A black cat used magic to open the door, so the kids got out. They went back to the deck and got candy."*

|  |  | Beginning 1 | Developing 2 | Proficient 3 |
|---|---|---|---|---|
| Setting and Characters | | One main character with a reference to a general place or time and a problem that elicits a character's response, but one that is not directly related to the event | One main character with a specific name and reference(s) to specific places or times and at least one stated event or problem that elicits a character's response | More than one main character with specific names, references to specific places and times, and two or more distinct stated events or problems that elicit the characters' responses |
| Initiating Event and Actions | | One statement about the character's emotions or feelings but the responses are not related to an event or problem and one statement about how the character might solve the problem; however, the character's actions are not related to the problem itself | One or more statements about the character's emotions or feelings related to an event or problem and two statements about how the character might solve the problem that includes attempts by the character to solve the problem | One or more statements about the character's emotions or feelings related to an event or problem and three or more statements about how the character might solve the problem that includes attempts by the character to solve the problem |
| Conclusion and Resolution | | One statement about what happened at the end of the story | One statement about what happened at the end of the story and how the character(s) felt as a result of the consequence | One statement about what happened at the end of the story including any additional problems/complications that occurred and how the character(s) felt as a result of the consequence |

| Date | Text | Setting and Characters | Initiating Event and Actions | Conclusion and Resolution | Total points |
|---|---|---|---|---|---|
| 1/10/2020 | A Sick Rock? | 1 | 1 | 1 | 3 |
| 2/10/2020 | In the Den | 2 | 2 | 1 | 5 |
| | | | | | |

## Sample student retelling set #2

1/10/2020 – Clouds and Rain – Student A

*"Clouds are in the sky. They are white. They are fluffy."*

|  | **Beginning** 1 | **Developing** 2 | **Proficient** 3 |
|---|---|---|---|
| Topic | No topic stated | General statement of topic | Precise label of topic |
| Major subtopic | No subtopics stated | Some subtopics stated | All subtopics stated |
| Supporting details | No supporting details included | Some supporting details included | All or most supporting details included |
| Language Usage | Little or no organization of information from the text selection | Information conveyed using some cohesive ties to show content relationship | Clear use of specific vocabulary and cohesive ties to convey the content information |

1/10/2020 – Clouds and Rain – Student B

*"Clouds are made of water. They can be white and fluffy. Some clouds are gray. These clouds make it rain."*

|  | **Beginning** 1 | **Developing** 2 | **Proficient** 3 |
|---|---|---|---|
| Topic | No topic stated | General statement of topic | Precise label of topic |
| Major subtopic | No subtopics stated | Some subtopics stated | All subtopics stated |
| Supporting details | No supporting details included | Some supporting details included | All or most supporting details included |

| | Beginning 1 | Developing 2 | Proficient 3 |
|---|---|---|---|
| Language Usage | Little or no organization of information from the text selection | Information conveyed using some cohesive ties to show content relationship | Clear use of specific vocabulary and cohesive ties to convey the content information |

## Student A

| Date | Text | Topic | Major subtopics | Supporting Details | Language Usage | Total points |
|---|---|---|---|---|---|---|
| 1/10/2020 | Clouds and Rain | 2 | 1 | 2 | 1 | 6 |
| | | | | | | |
| | | | | | | |

## Student B

| Date | Text | Topic | Major subtopics | Supporting Details | Language Usage | Total points |
|---|---|---|---|---|---|---|
| 1/10/2020 | Clouds and Rain | 2 | 2 | 3 | 3 | 10 |
| | | | | | | |
| | | | | | | |

## Possible Analysis for Try It! Cue Questions for Text Analysis (from page 77 – 78)

| Big Idea | Question |
|---|---|
| Cohesive ties | Are there causal, intentional or temporal connections in this micro-passage? |

#1  *How Do Seeds Grow?*

Many plants start out as small seeds. How does a seed grow?

First, it falls or is put into dirt. The sun's light helps the seed to grow. The seed gets energy from water.

Before long, the seed breaks open. Roots start to grow down into the dirt. Then a shoot pushes up through the dirt. The stem and leaves pop out next.

Soon, the little plant will be grown-up.

 What were we thinking?

The explicit use of words that signal a time sequence—**first, before long, then**, and **soon**—makes this a good micro-passage to illustrate this type of temporal cohesive ties.

.......

| Big Idea | Question |
|---|---|
| Background knowledge | What word/phrase is essential to understand the story? |

#2  *Starting Over*

Two girls in Sri Lanka walk past the rubble that was once their school. It was destroyed in the tsunami (soo-NAH-mee), **or** <u>series of huge waves</u>, that hit South Asia in December of 2005.

 What were we thinking?

Topic-specific vocabulary is the vehicle for building background knowledge. In this excerpt, the word **tsunami** is likely to be unfamiliar to students but is essential to understanding the passage.

Additionally, the new vocabulary word is defined within the text. Learning to use signal words (e.g., **or** – bold in text) can help students determine the meaning of the new terms (underlined in text).

.......

| **Big Idea** | **Question** |
|---|---|
| Inferential thinking | What gap did I need to fill to understand the text? |

#3     *The Hungry Girl*

"No! I'm hungry!"
Said the little girl
To her dearest dad

"Would you like some yummy yogurt?
<u>That's not what your brother had</u>."

<u>"Yes I would"</u>
Said the little girl
To her dearest dad
She ate the yogurt by herself,
<u>Which made her brother mad</u>!

     What were we thinking?

This poem gets its meaning—and humor—from the reader's prior experiential knowledge about the dynamics between siblings. The fact that the hungry girl would only eat something her brother hadn't eaten is based on knowledge of this type of dynamic.

Gap filled: The little girl didn't want to eat what her brother had as siblings often do to make each other upset.

.......

| **Big Idea** | **Question** |
|---|---|
| Reading/Writing connection | What namer (noun) and action (verb) can we use to write a sentence summary? |

#4     *A Butterfly's Life*

    A butterfly's life begins in a special way. First, a mother butterfly lays an egg on a leaf. A caterpillar hatches from the egg. The caterpillar eats leaves and grows bigger.

     What were we thinking?

Selecting **life** (namer) and **begins** (action) should guide students to write a summary sentence that uses the information in the micro-passage to expand the base sentence.

.......

| **Big Idea** | **Question** |
| --- | --- |
| Text Structure | How is the text organized? |

#5     *The Story of a Snowflake*

 What were we thinking?

First, drops of water in clouds get cold. Next, those drops turn into bits of ice. Then, the bits of ice stick together. They stick together in all kinds of shapes. The shapes get heavy. They fall from the clouds to the ground. We call these icy shapes snowflakes!

The explicit use of words that signal a time sequence—**first, next,** and **then**—signals text that is organized as a sequence of steps in a process. This is an indication that this text excerpt is informational rather than narrative in structure.

# Story Map (Stage 0)

# Narrative Story Map ( Stage 1)

Title_____ Author_____

**Setting**

**Characters**

**Initiating Event**

**Reaction/Feelings**

**Actions/Attempts**

**Consequence**

Adapted from map by Lorna Idol    Literacy How, Inc. 2009, 2020

# Narrative Story Map (Stage 2)

Title_____     Author_____

| Setting | Characters |

↓

| Initiating Event |

↓

| Reaction/Feelings | → | The Plan |

↓

| Actions/Attempts |

↓

| Consequence | Resolution |

Adapted from map by Lorna Idol     Literacy How, Inc. 2009, 2020

# Knowledge Tree

# Riddle Planning Guide

Use for Stage 1 **What Is It?** (See page 151)

|  | Literal clues |
|---|---|
| Category? |  |
| Color? |  |
| Shape? |  |
| Size? |  |
| Texture? |  |
| How move? |  |
| How used? |  |
| Behavior? |  |
|  |  |
|  |  |
| What am I? | ANSWER |

Use for Stage 2 **What Is It?** (See page 154)

|  | Literal clues | Figurative clues |
|---|---|---|
| Category? |  |  |
| Color? |  |  |
| Shape? |  |  |
| Size? |  |  |
| Texture? |  |  |
| How move? |  |  |
| How used? |  |  |
| Behavior? |  |  |
|  |  |  |
|  |  |  |
| What am I? |  | ANSWER |

# Text Selections for Reference and Practice

The following table lists the text selections provided for reference from the instructional activities and for additional practice for teachers. The text selections are listed in the order in which they appear in the activities.

| Text Title (page number) | Story Map | Knowledge Trees | Text Links | Use What You Know | Sentence Summaries | What's the Answer | Rubrics |
|---|---|---|---|---|---|---|---|
| *The Hungry Girl* (207) | 0[1] | | | | 0 | 0 | |
| *In the Den* (208) | 1 | | | 1 | 1 | 1 | √ |
| *Jack and the Beanstalk* (209) | 2 | | | 2 | 2 | 2 | |
| **Eat Right, Feel Great**[2] (212) | | 0 | | | | 0 | |
| **Celebrations Around the World**[2] (212) | | 1 | | | | 1 | |
| *How Do Seeds Grow* (213) | | 2 | | | | | √ |
| *Wind Helps Plants Grow* (213) | | 2 | | | | | √ |
| *Seeds Need to Move* (214) | | 2 | | | | | √ |
| *So Many Spices* (214) | | | | | 0 | | |
| *Chinese New Year* (215) | | | 1 | | 1 | | |
| *A Plant Puzzle* (215) | | | 2 | | 2 | 2 | |
| *Clouds and Rain* (216) | | | | | | | √ |
| *A Sick Rock?* (217) | | | | | | | √ |

[1]0, 1 and 2 refer to the stage in which the text is used for the activity.

[2]For the titles in bold, the link to these text selections are provided rather than in print.

# The Hungry Girl

"I'm hungry!"
Said the little girl
To her dearest dad
"Would you like to sip some soup?
That's what your brother had."

"No! I'm hungry!"
Said the little girl
To her dearest dad
"Would you like to taste this toast?
That's what your brother had."

"No! I'm hungry!"
Said the little girl
To her dearest dad
"Would you like to munch a muffin?
That's what your brother had."

"No! I'm hungry!"
Said the little girl
To her dearest dad
"Would you like some yummy yogurt?
That's *not* what your brother had."

"Yes I would!"
Said the little girl
To her dearest dad.
She ate the yogurt by herself,
Which made her brother mad!

Used with permission from www.ReadWorks.org

# In the Den

1. On the deck, the kids had bags.
   A mom had a black hat.
   She said, "Pick gum and pops for your bags."

2. It was lots of fun for the kids!
   Tim had a big fin and a wig.
   Liz and Ann had rad wigs.

3. The mom gives the kids and Tim a pass to go to a den.
   The den was not lit.
   It was dim in the den.

4. Tim, Liz, and Ann can not see.
   A rat fell on Tim's back.
   He yells, "Aaaaa! My back!"

5. Tim, Ann, and Liz run.
   Ann Yells, "Aaaaa!"
   She said to Liz, "A web is on your neck."

6. The kids began to yell, "Let's go back!"
   But it's so dim.
   The kids can not see.

7. Liz, Tim, and Ann yell, "We want to go!"
   But a bat hit Ann's leg.
   She yells, "Aaaaa!"

8. The kids want to go back to the deck.
   But the lock has a jam.
   No! No! No! The kids sat and sat.

9. Tick-tock. Tick-tock.
   "We have to fix the lock!"
   Tim and the kids give the lock a big tug.

10. The kids do not have good luck.
    Liz, Ann, and Tim can not pick the lock.
    The kids yell, "Get us! We are not O.K."

11. A black cat rubs on Ann's back.
    Prrrrrr....
    The cat said, "I can pick the lock."

12. The kids tell the cat, "A black cat is bad luck."
    The cat said, "Not me. I am good luck.
    You can not see me pick the lock. But I will."

13. Wam. Zam. Bam!
    Fog fills the den.
    The kids and Tim can not see the black cat pick the lock.

14. Wam. Zam. Bam!
    The kids and Tim are on the deck.
    Tim, Liz, and Ann do not see the black cat.

15. Tim and the kids see gum and pops on the deck.
    The kids said, "Yes! The black cat is good luck.
    She got us back."

16. The kids and Tim pick lots of gum and pops. Yum!
    Liz, Ann, and Tim have fun on the deck.
    A black cat can be good luck.

Used with permission from J. Lauren
www.whole-phonics.com

# Jack and the Beanstalk

Once upon a time there lived a poor widow who had an only son named Jack. She was very poor, for times had been hard, and Jack was too young to work. Almost all the furniture of the little cottage had been sold to buy bread, until at last there was nothing left worth selling.

Only the good cow, Milky White, remained, and she gave milk every morning, which they took to market and sold. But one sad day Milky White gave no milk, and then things looked bad indeed.

"Never mind, mother," said Jack. "We must sell Milky White. Trust me to make a good bargain," and away he went to the market.

For some time he went along very sadly, but after a little he quite recovered his spirits. "I may as well ride as walk," said he; so instead of leading the cow by the halter, he jumped on her back, and so he went whistling along until he met a butcher.

"Good morning," said the butcher.

"Good morning, sir," answered Jack.

"Where are you going?" said the butcher.

"I am going to market to sell the cow."

"It's lucky I met you," said the butcher. "You may save yourself the trouble of going so far."

With this, he put his hand in his pocket, and pulled out five curious-looking beans. "What do you call these?" he said.

"Beans," said Jack.

"Yes," said he, "beans, but they're the most wonderful beans that ever were known. If you plant them overnight, by the next morning they'll grow up and reach the sky. But to save you the trouble of going all the way to market, I don't mind exchanging them for that cow of yours."

"Done!" cried Jack, who was so delighted with the bargain that he ran all the way home to tell his mother how lucky he had been.

But oh! how disappointed the poor widow was.

"Off to bed with you!" she cried; and she was so angry that she threw the beans out of the window into the garden. So poor Jack went to bed without any supper, and cried himself to sleep.

When he woke up the next morning, the room was almost dark; and Jack jumped out of bed and ran to the window to see what was the matter. The sun was shining brightly outside, but from the ground right up beside his window there was growing a great beanstalk, which stretched up and up as far as he could see, into the sky.

"I'll just see where it leads to," thought Jack, and with that he stepped out of the window on to the beanstalk, and began to climb upwards. He climbed up and up, till after a time his mother's cottage looked a mere speck below, but at last the stalk ended, and he found himself in a new and beautiful country. A little way off there was a great castle, with a broad road leading straight up to the front gate.

But what most surprised Jack was to find a beautiful maiden suddenly standing beside him. "Good morning, ma'am," said he, very politely.

"Good morning, Jack," said she; and Jack was more surprised than ever, for he could not imagine how she had learned his name. But he soon found that she knew a great deal more about him than his name; for she told him how, when he was quite a little baby, his father, a gallant knight, had been slain by the giant who lived in yonder castle, and how his mother, in order to save Jack, had been obliged to promise never to tell the secret.

"All that the giant has is yours," she said, and then disappeared quite as suddenly as she came.

"She must be a fairy," thought Jack.

As he drew near to the castle, he saw the giant's wife standing at the door.

"If you please, ma'am," said he, "would you kindly give me some breakfast? I have had nothing to eat since yesterday."

Now, the giant's wife, although very big and very ugly, had a kind heart, so she said: "Very well, little man, come in; but you must be quick about it, for if my husband, the giant, finds you here, he will eat you up, bones and all."

So in Jack went, and the giant's wife gave him a good breakfast, but before he had half finished it there came a terrible knock at the front door, which seemed to shake even the thick walls of the castle.

"Dearie me, that is my husband!" said the giantess, in a terrible fright; "we must hide you somehow," and she lifted Jack up and popped him into the empty kettle.

No sooner had the giant's wife opened the door than her husband roared out: "Fee, fi, fo, fum,

I smell the blood of an Englishman; Be he alive, or be he dead,
I'll grind his bones to make my bread!"

"It's a boy, I'm sure it is," he continued. "Where is he? I'll have him for my breakfast."

"Nonsense!" said his wife; "you must be mistaken. It's the ox's hide you smell." So he sat down, and ate up the greater part of the ox. When he had finished he said: "Wife, bring me my money- bags." So his wife brought him two full bags of gold, and the giant began to count his money. But he was so sleepy that his head soon began to nod, and then he began to snore, like the rumbling of thunder. Then Jack crept out, snatched up the two bags, and though the giant's dog barked loudly, he made his way down the beanstalk back to the cottage before the giant awoke.

Jack and his mother were now quite rich; but it occurred to him one day that he would like to see how matters were going on at the giant's castle. So while his mother was away at market, he climbed up, and up, and up, and up, until he got to the top of the beanstalk again.

The giantess was standing at the door, just as before, but she did not know Jack, who, of course, was more finely dressed than on his first visit. "If you please, ma'am," said he, "will you give me some breakfast?"

"Run away," said she, "or my husband the giant will eat you up, bones and all. The last boy who came here stole two bags of gold-- off with you!" But the giantess had a kind heart, and after a time she allowed Jack to come into the kitchen, where she set before him enough breakfast to last him a week. Scarcely had he begun to eat than there was a great rumbling like an earthquake, and the giantess had only time to bundle Jack into the oven when in came the giant. No sooner was he inside the room than he roared:

"Fee, fi, fo, fum,
I smell the blood of an Englishman; Be he alive, or be he dead,
I'll grind his bones to make my bread!"

But his wife told him he was mistaken, and after breakfasting off a roasted bullock, just as if it were a lark, he called out: "Wife, bring the little brown hen!" The giantess went out and brought in a little brown hen, which she placed on the table.

"Lay!" said the giant; and the hen at once laid a golden egg. "Lay!" said the giant a second time; and she laid another golden egg. "Lay!" said the giant a third time; and she laid a third golden egg.

"That will do for to-day," said he, and stretched himself out to go to sleep. As soon as he began to snore, Jack crept out of the oven, went on tiptoe to the table, and, snatching up the little brown hen, made a dash for the door. Then the hen began to

cackle, and the giant began to wake up; but before he was quite awake, Jack had escaped from the castle, and, climbing as fast as he could down the beanstalk, got safe home to his mother's cottage.

The little brown hen laid so many golden eggs that Jack and his mother had now more money than they could spend. But Jack was always thinking about the beanstalk; and one day he crept out of the window again, and climbed up, and up, and up, and up, until he reached the top.

This time, you may be sure, he was careful not to be seen; so he crept round to the back of the castle, and when the giant's wife went out he slipped into the kitchen and hid himself in the oven. In came the giant, roaring louder than ever:

"Fee, fi, fo, fum,
I smell the blood of an Englishman; Be he alive; or be he dead,
I'll grind his bones to make my bread!"

But the giantess was quite sure that she had seen no little boys that morning; and after grumbling a great deal, the giant sat down to breakfast. Even then he was not quite satisfied, for every now and again he would say:

"Fee, fi, fo, fum,
I smell the blood of an Englishman;" and once he got up and looked in the kettle. But, of course, Jack was in the oven all the time!

When the giant had finished, he called out: "Wife, bring me the golden harp!" So she brought in the golden harp, and placed it on the table. "Sing!" said the giant; and the harp at once began to sing the most beautiful songs that ever were heard. It sang so sweetly that the giant soon fell fast asleep; and then Jack crept quietly out of the oven, and going on tiptoe to the table, seized hold of the golden harp. But the harp at once called out: "Master! master!" and the giant woke up just in time to catch sight of Jack running out of the kitchen-door.

With a fearful roar, he seized his oak-tree club, and dashed after Jack, who held the harp tight, and ran faster than he had ever run before. The giant, brandishing his club, and taking terribly long strides, gained on Jack at every instant, and he would have been caught if the giant hadn't slipped over a boulder. Before he could pick himself up, Jack began to climb down the beanstalk, and when the giant arrived at the edge he was nearly half-way to the cottage. The giant began to climb down too; but as soon as Jack saw him coming, he called out: "Mother, bring me an axe!" and the widow hurried out with a chopper. Jack had no sooner reached the ground than he cut the beanstalk right in two. Down came the giant with a terrible crash, and that, you may be sure, was the end of him. What became of the giantess and the castle nobody knows. But Jack and his mother grew very rich, and lived happy ever after.

*Eat Right, Feel Great!* www.ReadWorks.org

*Celebrations Around the World* www.ReadWorks.org

## How Do Seeds Grow?

### by ReadWorks

Many plants start out as small seeds. How does a seed grow?

First, a seed falls or is put into dirt. Water and the sun's light might help the seed to start growing.

Soon, the seed breaks open. Roots start to grow down into the dirt. Then a shoot pushes up through the dirt. The stem and leaves pop out next.

Soon, the little plant will be grown-up.

## Wind Helps Plants Grow

### by Linda Ruggieri

Wind is air that moves. When air moves, it blows things from one place to another.

Wind blows seeds around. That allows new plants to grow. Think about the dandelion flower. Have you ever seen one that has turned white? Inside it are seeds. When wind blows on a white dandelion, its seeds float away.

Some of those seeds will fall on the ground. Soon, something will change in the place where the wind blew the seeds. New dandelion plants will grow there!

## Seeds Need to Move

by Rachelle Kreisman

A plant starts life as a seed. When that seed grows into a plant, that plant makes new seeds. Those seeds, too, can grow and turn into more new plants.

But did you know that not every seed grows into a plant? To become a plant, a seed has to travel. That is because seeds need room to grow. A seed has to be far enough away from other plants so that it gets the sunlight and water it needs. If a seed falls to the ground too close to its parent plant, it may not grow.

Of course, wind can spread the seeds for many plants. But some plants depend on animals to move their seeds. Those seeds are called hitchhiker seeds. They travel on something else that moves!

Many hitchhiker seeds are prickly. They have tiny rows of hooks. The hooks can stick to fur or feathers. Hitchhiker seeds can travel for miles on an animal's body. Then they fall off or are removed. If they fall in a place that is good for growing, the seeds will grow into plants, too!

Used with permission from www.ReadWorks.org

## So Many Spices

Lots of foods have their own flavor. But some of them have weak flavors. They don't taste like much. So what do people do when they want to add more flavor to a food? They can add spices!

A spice is something that's used to give flavor to foods. Spices come from different parts of different plants. Some spices are seeds. These include sesame, poppy, and cumin. Other spices come from tree bark. Cinnamon is a spice that comes from the bark of a tree. And some spices come from fruits. Pepper is a spice that comes from a fruit. To make pepper, people dry out a berry called a peppercorn. Then they grind it up!

Spices are popular all over the world. But many spices are only grown in warm, wet places. Lots of them are grown in south and east Asia. Long ago, this meant that people from Europe had to travel or trade to get the spices they wanted. Explorers sailed across oceans to get to the areas that grew spices.

Today, it's a lot easier to get spices from all over the world. That's something to be happy about the next time you add pepper to your meal!

Used with permission from www.ReadWorks.org

**Chinese New Year**

by Cecilia Na

The Chinese New Year is an important holiday celebrated by Chinese people all around the world. During this time, Chinese families get together to spend time with one another. Together, they celebrate the past year. They also wish each other good luck for the New Year.

The date of the Chinese New Year changes every year. However, it always falls some time between January 20 and February 21. This is because the Chinese culture used to follow a calendar called the Chinese Lunar Calendar. This calendar is different from the calendar used in the United States of America. This calendar is called the Gregorian calendar.

Like many holidays, there are traditions people have to celebrate the Chinese New Year. For this holiday, many people wear red. They even put up red decorations. In Chinese culture, the color red stands for good luck. Another important tradition is the gift of a red envelope called 'hongbao.' The elderly put money inside the 'hongbao' and give it to children to wish them good fortune.

Used with permission from www.ReadWorks.org

**A Plant Puzzle**

By Josh Adler

Living things like plants, animals, and people need energy to survive and grow. People eat food for energy, but most plants use energy that they get from sunlight.

When you look at plants such as a tree, flower, or grass, what do you see?

You might notice their stems, trunks, branches, leaves, roots, or flowers, but how do they grow? What are they made from? How did the plant make those parts?

Life is a puzzle in many ways. People don't all agree on how life started or why it exists. Yet a simple way of thinking about how plants grow is to think of the plant itself as a piece of a larger puzzle.

Each plant is a part of its unique environment. Different environments could be oceans, forests, deserts, or cities. Each environment also has its own climate, which is partially based on how much sun and rain an area receives every year.

Since only certain plants grow in hot, cool, wet, or dry climates, each environment is made up of different types of plant life. A desert may grow palm trees and cacti, while a forest may grow tall pines or oak trees.

In order for a plant to grow, it needs three very important puzzle pieces: water, carbon dioxide, and light. Plants use their roots to take in water from the ground. They use their leaves to take in sunlight and carbon dioxide from the air.

Plants use these three puzzle pieces to make their own food in a process called photosynthesis. Using the energy from the sun, plants convert water and carbon dioxide into sugar. This sugar feeds the plant's growth from a seedling into an adult. In the process, the plant releases oxygen into the air.

Another important piece to the growth of many plants is soil. Using their roots, plants take in nutrients from the soil that help them grow. Giving a plant a spot in clean soil is important to make sure it doesn't absorb anything harmful from the dirt.

Plants make their food from carbon dioxide, water and light. They use this food to grow stems, trunks, roots, branches, leaves, and flowers. Now when you look at a tree, flower, or even a blade of grass, you can see all the pieces of the plant and how the entire puzzle fits together.

## Clouds and Rain

Look up at the sky. You may see clouds. What are clouds made of?

Clouds are made of tiny drops of water. Some clouds look white and fluffy. Some clouds look stringy, like wisps of hair. Other clouds look gray.

Gray clouds can bring rain. They are made of bigger drops of water. If the drops get too big, they fall from the sky. Now it is raining.

# A Sick Rock?

1. Nick and Meg are on a dock.
   Nick tags Meg. She tags Nick.
   The kids have lots of fun.

2. Nick fell on a big rock.
   "Quick! My neck!" yells Nick.
   Meg ran to pick him up.
   "Are you O.K.?" she said.

3. "Yes, but I want to pick up the rock,"
   said Nick.
   "A rock can not be on a dock."
   The kids get the rock.

4. The rock was a mess!
   It had muck on it.
   "Yuck!" said Meg.
   Oh no! The rock began to kick!

5. Nick and Meg see it is not a rock.
   It's a duck, and it is sick.

6. Nick runs to get a sack.
   The sick duck began to peck and quack.
   A vet will have to fix the duck.

7. Meg ran to get Zac and his van.
   The kids and the duck get in the back of
   the van.
   Zac zips to the vet.

8. The kids lug the sack in to see the vet.
   Meg's dad is the vet.
   Dad sees the duck and yells, "Yuck! The
   rock has muck on it.

9. Meg said, "Dad! Do not be mad at us.
   It's a sick duck! You are a vet.
   We want you to fix him."

10. Dad can fix the duck.
    He wants to rub the muck off the duck.
    But, the duck began to peck at Dad.

11. The muck got on Nick, Meg, and Dad.
    Meg runs to get a rag and suds.

12. The duck loves the suds.
    Nick and Meg love the suds.
    The suds rock!

13. The duck is not sick.
    The duck wants to go back to the dock.
    But he can not go back to the muck.

14. Dad has to go and fix a sick cat.
    Meg and Nick see Zac in the van.

15. The duck has luck.
    He can go to the zoo.
    Meg, Nick, and the duck get in the van.

16. Zac zips the van to the zoo.
    Meg and Nick hug the duck and tell him,
    "Lots of luck!"

Used with permission from J. Lauren
www.whole-phonics.com

# References and Resources

Abadiano, H. R. & Turner, J. (2003). The RAND report: Reading for understanding: Toward an R&D program in reading comprehension. *New England Reading Association Journal 39*(2), 74.

Beck, I. L. & McKeown, M. G. (1981). Developing questions that promote comprehension: The story map. *Language Arts 58*(8), 913-918.

Beck, I. & McKeown, M. (1986). Instructional research in reading: A retrospective. *Reading comprehension: From research to practice*, 113-134.

Beck, I. L. & McKeown, M. G. (2001). Text talk: Capturing the benefits of read-aloud experiences for young children. *The Reading Teacher 55*(1), 10-20.

Beck, I. L. & McKeown, M. G. (2002). Questioning the author: Making sense of social studies. *Educational Leadership 59*(3).

Berninger, V. W. & Winn, W. (2006). Implications of advancements in brain research and technology for writing development, writing instruction, and educational evolution. *Handbook of writing research*, 96-114.

Bittner, M. (2004). *The Wild Parrots of Telegraph Hill*. Three Rivers Press: New York.

Cain, K. (2009). Making sense of text: Skills that support text comprehension and its development. *Perspectives on Language and Literacy 35*(2), 11-14.

Cain, K. & Oakhill, J. (2007). Cognitive bases of children's language comprehension difficulties. *Children's comprehension problems in oral and written language: A cognitive perspective*, 283. New York: Guilford Press.

Cain, K. & Oakhill, J. (2009). Reading comprehension development from 8 to 14 years. *Beyond decoding: The behavioral and biological foundations of reading comprehension*, 143-175. New York: Guilford Press.

Cain, K. & Nash, H. M. (2011). The influence of connectives on young readers' processing and comprehension of text. *Journal of Educational Psychology 103*(2), 429.

Carlisle, J. & Rice, M. S. (2002). *Improving reading comprehension: Research-based principles and practices*. Timonium, MD: York Press.

Carnine, D. & Kinder, D. (1985). Teaching low-performing students to apply generative and schema strategies to narrative and expository material. *Remedial and Special Education 6*(1), 20-30.

Carreker, S. (2011). Necessities for critical reading: Skilled decoding and language comprehension. Bellaire, TX: Neuhaus Education Center.

Cartwright, K. B. (2012). Insights from cognitive neuroscience: The importance of executive function for early reading development and education. *Early Education & Development 23*(1), 24-36.

Cartwright, K. B. (2015). *Executive skills and reading comprehension: A guide for educators*. New York: The Guilford Press.

Castles, A., Rastle, K., & Nation, K. (2018). "Ending the reading wars: Reading acquisition from novice to expert": Corrigendum.

Catts, H. W. & Kamhi, A. G. (1999). Causes of reading disabilities. *Language and reading disabilities*, 95-127.

Chall, J. S. (1967). *The great debate*. McGraw-Hill: New York.

Chall, J. S. (1983). *Stages of reading development*. McGraw-Hill: New York.

Chapel, J. M. & Eberhardt, N. C. (2011). *What's Different…What's the Same?* Rowe Publishing & Design: Kansas.

Demi (1990). *The Empty Pot*. New York: Square Fish, an imprint of MacMillan.

Dewitz, P., Carr, E., & Patberg, J. (1987). Effects of inference training on comprehension and comprehension monitoring. *Reading Research Quarterly 22*, 99-121.

Dillon, C. M., 2009. *See It Again for the First Time*. Yale-New Haven Teachers' Institute.

Drymock, S. (2007). Comprehension Strategy Instruction: Teaching Narrative Text Structure Awareness, *The Reading Teacher 61*(2), pp. 161-167.

Duke, N. K. (2014). *Inside Information: Developing Powerful Readers and Writers of Informational Text Through Project-Based Instruction*. Scholastic: New York.

Duke, N. K. (2016). Project-Based Instruction: A Great Match for Informational Texts. *American Educator 40*(3), 4.

Dyer, J. R., Shatz, M., & Wellman, H. M. (2000). Young children's storybooks as a source of mental state information. *Cognitive Development 15*(1), 17-37.

Eberhardt, N. C. (2013). Syntax: Somewhere between words and text. *Perspectives on Language and Literacy 39*(3), 44-49.

Elbro, C. & Buch-Iverson, I. (2013). Activation of background knowledge for inference making: Effects on reading comprehension. *Scientific Studies of Reading 17*, 435-452.

Elleman, A. M. & Compton, D. L. (2017). Beyond Comprehension Strategy Instruction: What's Next? Language, Speech, and Hearing Services in Schools. Vol. 48, 84-91.

Fisher. D. & Frey, N. (2014). Speaking and listening in content area learning. *The Reading Teacher 68*(1), 64 – 69 doi: 10.1002/trtr.1296

Fisher, D., Frey, N., & Hattie, J. (2016) Visible Learning or Literacy Implementing the Practices that Work Best to Accelerate Student Learning.

Florit, E., Roch, M., & Levorato, M. C. (2013). The relationship between listening comprehension of text and sentences in preschoolers: Specific or mediated by lower and higher level components? *Applied Psycholinguistics 34*(2), 395-415.

Gersten, R., Fuchs, L. S., Williams, J. P., & Baker, S. (2001). Teaching reading comprehension strategies to students with learning disabilities: A review of research. *Review of Educational Research 71*(2), 279-320.

Gough, P. B. & Tunmer, W. E. (1986). Decoding, reading, and reading disability. *Remedial and Special Education 7*(1), 6-10.

Graesser, A. C. & Clark, L. F. (1985). *Structures and procedures of implicit knowledge* (Vol. 17). Ablex Publishing Corporation.

Graesser, A. C., Singer, M., & Trabasso, T. (1994). Constructing inferences during narrative text comprehension. *Psychological Review 101*(3), 371.

Graesser, A. C., McNamara, D. S., & Louwerse, M. M. (2003). What do readers need to learn in order to process coherence relations in narrative and expository text. *Rethinking reading comprehension*, 82-98.

Graham, S. & Hebert, M. (2010). *Writing to read: Evidence for how writing can improve reading*. Washington, DC: Alliance for Excellent Education.

Graham, S. & Hebert, M. (2011). Writing to read: A meta-analysis of the impact of writing and writing instruction on reading. *Harvard Educational Review 81*(4), 710-744.

Hirsch, E. D., Jr. (Summer, 2003). Reading comprehension requires knowledge—of words and the world. *American Educator 27* (1), 10-22, 28-29, 44.

Hochman, J. C. & Wexler, N. (2017). *The writing revolution: A guide to advancing thinking through writing in all subjects and grades*. Josey-Bass: San Francisco.

Hochman, J. C. & Wexler, N. (2019). The connections between writing, knowledge acquisition, and reading comprehension. *Perspectives on Language and Literacy 45*(4), 25 – 29.

Hogan, T., Bridges, M. S., Justice, L.M., & Cain, K. (2011). Increasing higher level language skills to improve reading comprehension. *Focus on Exceptional Children 44* (3), 1-20.

Hoover, W. A., & Gough, P. B. (1990). The simple view of reading. *Reading and Writing 2*(2), 127-160.

How Do Seeds Grow? www.Readwords.org

Hughes, C. D. (2013). *National Geographic Little Kids First Big Book of the Ocean*. Washington, DC: National Geographic Society.

Hulme, C. & Snowling, M. J. (2016). Reading disorders and dyslexia. *Current Opinion in Pediatrics 28*(6), 731.

Jackson, G. T., Allen, L. K., & McNamara, D. S. (2016). COMMON CORE TERA. *Adaptive Educational Technologies for Literacy Instruction*, 49.

Jackson, G. T., Allen, L. K., & McNamara, D. S. (2016). Common Core TERA: Text Ease and Readability Assessor. In D. S. McNamara & S. A. Crossley (Eds.) *Adaptive educational technologies for literacy instruction* (pp.49-68). Taylor & Francis, Routledge: NY.

Jennings, T. M. & Haynes, C. W. (2018). *From Talking to Writing: Strategies for Supporting Narrative and Expository Writing*. Prides Crossing, MA: Landmark School Outreach Program.

Kamhi, A. G. & Catts, H. W. (2017). Epilogue: Reading comprehension is not a single ability—Implications for Assessment and Instruction. *Language, Speech, and Hearing Services in Schools 48*(2), 104-107.

Kintsch, W. & Van Dijk, T. A. (1978). Toward a model of text comprehension and production. *Psychological Review 85*(5), 363.

Kintsch, W. & Walter Kintsch, C. B. E. M. A. F. R. S. (1998). *Comprehension: A paradigm for cognition*. Cambridge University Press.

Langston, M. C., Trabasso, T., & Magliano, J. P. (1998). Modeling on-line comprehension. *Computational models of reading and understanding*, 181-225.

Lauren, J. (2018). *Buzz, Buzz*. www.WholePhonics.com.

Lepola, J., Lynch, J., Laakkonen, E., Silvén, M., & Niemi, P. (2012). The role of inference making and other language skills in the development of narrative listening comprehension in 4–6-year-old children. *Reading Research Quarterly 47*(3), 259-282.

Liben, D. & Davidson, B. (2019). What a knowledge-building approach looks like in the classroom. *Perspectives on Language and Literacy 45*(4), 31-35.

McCabe, M. (2011). English-language learners. *Education Week*.

McNamara, D. S., & Kintsch, W. (1996). Learning from texts: Effects of prior knowledge and text coherence. *Discourse Processes 22*(3), 247-288.

McNamara, D. S., Ozuru, Y., & Floyd, R. (2011). Comprehension challenges in the fourth grade: The roles of text cohesion, text genre, and readers' prior knowledge. *International Electronic Journal of Elementary Education 4(1), 229-257.*

McNamara, D. S. & Kendeou, P. (2011). Translating advances in reading comprehension research to educational practice. *International Electronic Journal of Elementary Education 4*(1), 33-46.

McNamara, D. S., Graesser, A. C., McCarthy, P., & Cai, Z. (2014). *Automated evaluation of text and discourse with Coh-Metrix*. Cambridge: Cambridge University Press.

Marzano, R. J. (2010). The art and science of teaching inference. *Educational Leadership 67*(7), 80 – 81.

Mesmer, A. E. (2017). *Teaching skills for complex text: Deepening close teaching in the classroom*. New York: Teachers College Press.

Moreau, M. R., Zagula, S. R., & Moreau, S. M. (2016). *The Critical Thinking Triangle in Action*. Springfield, MA: MindWing Concepts.

National Commission on Writing (2006). Writing and School reform. Available at www.collegeboard.com.

Neuman, S. B. (2019). Comprehension in disguise: The role of knowledge in children's learning. *Perspectives on Language and Literacy 45*(4), 12-16.

Oakhill, J. & Yuill, N. (1996). Reading comprehension difficulties. *Children's comprehension problems in oral and written language*, p. 41. New York: Guilford Press.

Oakhill, J. & Yuill, N. (1996). Higher order factors in comprehension disability: Processes and remediation. In C. Cornoldi & J. Oakhill (Eds.), *Reading comprehension difficulties; Processes and intervention*. (pp. 69 – 92). Mahwah, NJ: Erlbaum.

Oakhill, J., Cain, K. & Elbro, C. (2015) *Understanding and teaching reading comprehension: A handboo*k. New York: Routledge.

Odegard, T. N. (2019). Dyslexia defined: An update with implications for practice. *Perspectives on Language and Literacy 45*(1), 7-9.

Petersen, D. B., Gillam, S. L., & Gillam, R. B. (2008). Emerging Procedures in Narrative Assessment: The Index of Narrative Complexity. *Topics in Language Disorders 28*, 115-130.

Pressley, M. & Afflerbach, P. (1995). Verbal protocols of reading.

Recht, D. R. and Leslie, L. (1988) Effect of Prior Knowledge on Good and Poor Readers' Memory of Text. *Journal of Educational Psychology 80*(1), 16-20.

Scarborough, H. S. (2001). Connecting early language and literacy to later reading (dis)abilities: Evidence, theory, and practice. In S. Neuman & D. Dickinson (Eds.), *Handbook for research in early literacy* (pp. 97-110). New York: Guilford Press.

Schleppegrell, M. J. (2013). The role of metalanguage in supporting academic language development. *Language Learning, 63*, 153-170.

Schleppegrell, M. J. (2013) Exploring Language and Meaning in Complex Texts. *Perspectives on Language and Literacy 39*(3), 37-40.

Scott, C. M. (2009). A case for the sentence in reading comprehension. *Language, Speech, and Hearing Services in Schools* 40(2), 184-191.

Sedita, J. (2019). The strands that are woven into skilled writing. Rowley, MA: Keys to Literacy. Retrieved from: https://4eiav7adx2b1gsx1llq9qcln-wpengine.netdna-ssl.com/wp-content/uploads/2020/01/The-Strands-That-Are-Woven-Into-Skilled-Writing.pdf

Spear-Swerling, L. (2018). Learning Disabilities and Future Education Policy. *Perspectives on Learning Disabilities: Biological, Cognitive, Contextual*, 250.

Stafford, K. B., Williams, J. P., Nubla-Kung, A., & Pollini, S. (2005). Teaching at-risk second graders text structure via social studies content. *Teaching Exceptional Children, 38*(2), 62.

Stricht, T. G., & James, J.H. (1984). Listening and reading. In P.D. Pearson, R. Barr, M.L. Kamil, & P. Mosenthal (Eds.), *Handbook of Reading Research* (Vol. 1, pp. 293–317). White Plains, NY: Longman.

The Reading League. (2019, January 18). *Deciphering Decodable Text*. [Video file]. https://www.youtube.com/watch?v=74WdYxBczak&t=199s

Westby, C. E., & Clauser, P. S. (1999). The right stuff for writing: Assessing and facilitating written language. *Language and reading disabilities*, 259-324.

Westby, C. & Culatta, B. (2016). *Telling tales; Personal event narratives and life stories*. LSHSS. ASHA.

Westby, C. E. (2005). Assessing and remediating text comprehension problems. *Language and reading disabilities*, 157-232.

Wexler, N. (2019). *The Knowledge Gap: The Hidden cause of America's Broken Education System—and How to Fix It*. Avery: New York.

Wexler, N. (2019) Why We're Teaching Reading Comprehension in A Way That Doesn't Work. *Forbes* online.

Wexler, N. (2018). Why American Students Haven't Gotten Better at Reading in 20 Years. (https://www.theatlantic.com/education/archive/2018/04/-american-students-reading/557915/

Williams, J. P. (2005). Instruction in reading comprehension for primary-grade students: A focus on text structure. *The Journal of Special Education 39*(1), 6-18.

Willingham, D. T. (2006). The usefulness of brief instruction in reading comprehension strategies. *American Educator 30*(4), 39-50.

Willingham, D. T. (2006). How knowledge helps: It speeds and strengthens reading comprehension, learning—and thinking. *American Education 30*(1), 30-37.

Willingham, D. T. (2017). *The reading mind: A cognitive approach to understanding how the mind reads*. San Francisco, CA: John Wiley & Sons.

Willingham, D. T. & Lovette, G. (2014). Can Reading Comprehension Be Taught? *Teachers College Record,* Date Published: September 26, 2014 http://www.tcrecord.org.proxy.its.virginia.edu ID Number 17701, Date Accessed: 10/14/2014

Wright, T. S. (2019). Reading to learn from the start: The power of interactive read-alouds. *American Educator 42*(4).

Yuill, N. & Oakhill, J. (1988). Effects of inference awareness training on poor reading comprehension. *Applied Cognitive Psychology 2*(1), 33-45.

Made in the USA
Middletown, DE
05 September 2024

60395401R00126